The Classical Language of Architecture

JOHN SUMMERSON

The Classical Language of Architecture

The MIT Press

Massachusetts Institute of Technology

Cambridge, Massachusetts

Twentieth printing, 2001

ISBN 0 262 69012 8 (paperback)

Library of Congress Catalog Card Number 66-24572

Printed and bound in the United States of America.

Contents

Preface

A script written for broadcasting is a script written for broadcasting and it is, I think, a mistake to try to turn it into something else.
This book consists, therefore, of the very slightly revised scripts of
six talks, written for the B.B.C. and delivered in May-July 1963,
together with the illustrative material made available to listeners
in a booklet issued at the time. In preparing the talks, I had in
mind the non-professional student who is attracted by the history
of architecture and perhaps approaches it as part of a History of
Art course, but never quite grasps the grammatical discipline which
is the nerve of all classical architecture and some feeling for which
helps to illuminate most other architectures. To him (or her) and
to anybody who likes architecture well enough to want to start
thinking about it – instead of just gazing – this book is offered.

J.S.

1. The Essentials of Classicism

I must begin by assuming some general knowledge. Like, for instance, knowing that St. Paul's Cathedral is a classical building while Westminster Abbey is not; that the British Museum is a classical building while the Natural History Museum at South Kensington is not. That all the buildings round Trafalgar Square – the National Gallery, St. Martin's-in-the-Fields, Canada House and even (just) South Africa House are classical, that all the public buildings in White-hall are classical; but that the Houses of Parliament are not. Elementary distinctions, and you may think at once that I am going to deal in superficialities. When is a classical building not a classical building? Does it really matter? Are not the important qualities of architecture deeper than and independent of such stylistic nomenclature? They are. Nevertheless, I cannot reach all the things I want to say in these talks without first isolating all the buildings which are, *prima facie*, classical from all the others. I shall be talking about architecture as a language and all I want to assume at the moment is that you do recognize the Latin of architecture when you hear – that is, see – it.

The *Latin* of Architecture – that brings me to another general knowledge assumption. Classical architecture has its roots in antiquity, in the worlds of Greece and Rome, in the temple architecture of the Greek world and in the religious, military and civil architecture of the Romans. But these talks are not going to be about the architecture of Greece and Rome – they are not going to be about the growth and development of the classical language of architecture but about its nature and its use – its use as the common architectural language, inherited from Rome, of nearly the whole civilized world in the five centuries between the Renaissance and our own time.

Very well – from now on we can be more precise. Let us look at this word 'classical' as applied to architecture. It is a mistake to try to define classicism. It has all sorts of useful meanings in different contexts and I propose to consider two meanings only, both of which will be useful throughout these talks. The first meaning is the most obvious. A classical building is one whose decorative elements derive directly or indirectly from the architectural vocabulary of the ancient world – the 'classical' world as it is often called: these elements are easily recognizable, as for example columns of five standard varieties, applied in standard ways; standard ways of treating door and window openings and gable ends and standard runs of mouldings applicable to all these things. Notwithstanding that all these 'standards' are continually departed from they do remain still recognizable as standards throughout all buildings that may be called classical in this sense.

That, I think, is one fair description of what classical architecture is, but it is only skin-deep; it enables you to recognize the 'uniform' worn by a certain category of buildings, the category we call classical. But it tells you nothing about the essence of classicism in architecture. Here, however, we have got to be rather careful. 'Essences' are very elusive and are often found, on enquiry, not to exist. Nevertheless, embedded in the history of classical architecture is a series of statements about the essentials of architecture and these are in agreement over a long period, to the extent that we may say that the aim of classical architecture has always been to achieve a demonstrable harmony of parts. Such harmony has been felt to reside in the buildings of antiquity and to be to a great extent 'built in' to the principal antique elements – especially to the five 'orders' to which we shall come presently. But it has also been considered in the abstract by a series of theoreticians who have demonstrated that harmony analogous to musical harmony in a structure is achieved by proportion, that is to say by ensuring that the ratios in a building are simple arithmetical functions and that the ratios of all parts of the building are either those same ratios or related to them in a direct way. A vast amount of pretentious nonsense has been written about proportion and I have no intention of getting involved in it. The Renaissance concept of proportion is fairly simple. The purpose of proportion is to establish harmony throughout a structure – a harmony which is made comprehensible either by the conspicuous use of one or more of the orders as dominant components or else simply by the use of dimensions involving the repetition of simple ratios. That is enough for us to go on with.

There is, however, one point about this rather abstract conception of what is classical and it may be put as a question. Is it possible, you may ask, for a building to display absolutely none of the trappings associated with classical architecture and still, by virtue of proportion alone, to qualify as a 'classical' building? The answer must, I think, be 'no'. You can say, in describing such a building, that its proportions are classical, but it is simply confusing and an abuse of terminology to say that it *is* classical. The porches of Chartres Cathedral are, in distribution and proportion, just about as classical as you can get, but nobody is ever going to call them anything but Gothic. And one could cite plenty of other examples of the Gothic system being closely analogous to the classical. It is, by the way, a great mistake to think of Gothic and Classic as *opposites*; they are very different but they are not opposites and they are not wholly unrelated. It is nineteenth-century romanticism which has made us put them in totally different psychological camps. People who say they 'prefer' Gothic to Classic or Classic to Gothic are, I suspect, usually the victims of this nineteenth-century misinterpretation. The fact is that the essentials of architecture – as expounded by the Renaissance theorists – are to be found expressed, consciously or unconsciously, throughout the architectures of the world. And while we must incorporate these essentials in our idea of what is classical we must also accept the fact that classical architecture is only recognizable as such when it contains some allusion, however slight, however vestigial, to the antique 'orders'. Such an allusion may be no more than some groove or projection which suggests the idea of a cornice or even a disposition of windows which suggests the ratio of pedestal to column, column to entablature. Some modern buildings – notably those of the late Auguste Perret and his imitators – are classical in this way: that is to say, they are thought out in modern materials but in a classical spirit and sealed as classical only by the tiniest allusive gestures. In the last talk in this series I shall have more to say about all this. In the meantime the thing which it is quite essential for us to understand before we go any further is this question of the orders – the 'Five Orders of Architecture'. Everybody has heard of them, but what exactly are they? Why are there five and not four, or sixteen or three hundred and twenty-six?

One thing at a time. First, what are the orders? On the endpaper of this book you will find a very clear diagram of the Doric order. It consists, you see, of a temple column standing on a pedestal and carrying on its head the architrave, frieze and cornice, those elements which are collectively called the entablature. Then, in Plates 1 and 2 you see the Doric order again, with its four companions; it is the second from the left, with the Tuscan to the left of it, the Ionic, Corinthian and Composite to the right. There are two sets here – one of 1540 on the left of the page (Plate 1), the other more than a hundred years later (Plate 2), but they are in principle the same thing. An 'order' is the 'column-and-superstructure' unit of a temple colonnade. It does not *have* to have a pedestal and often does not. It *does* have to have an entablature (columns are meaningless unless they support something) and the cornice represents the eaves of the building finishing off the slope of the roof.

Now, why are there five orders? This is a little more difficult and it is necessary to glance back to some origins. The earliest written description of any of the orders is in Vitruvius. The name of this Roman author will crop up frequently in these talks and this is the moment to introduce him. He was an architect of some consquence in the reign of Augustus and wrote a treatise in ten books: *De Architectura*, which he dedicated to the Emperor. This is the only treatise of its kind to have survived from antiquity and for that reason has been accorded enormous veneration. Vitruvius was not himself a man of any great genius or literary talent or indeed – for all we know – of architectural talent. The thing about his treatise is that it rounds up and preserves for us an immense quantity of traditional building lore – it is the code of practice of a Roman architect of the first century A.D. enriched with instances and historical notes.

In the course of Vitruvius' third and fourth books he describes three of the orders – Ionic, Doric and Corinthian – and gives a few notes on another, the Tuscan. He tells us in which part of the world each was invented. He relates them to his descriptions of temples and tells us to which Gods and Goddesses each order is appropriate. His descriptions are by no means exhaustive, he gives no fifth order, he does not present them in what we think of as the 'proper' sequence (Tuscan, Doric, Ionic, Corinthian) and – most important – he does not present them as a set of canonical formulae embodying all architectural virtue. That was left for the theorists of the Renaissance.

In the middle of the fifteenth century, fourteen hundred years after Vitruvius, the Florentine architect and humanist, Leon Battista Alberti, described the orders, partly with reference to Vitruvius and partly from his own observations of Roman remains. It was he who added, from observation, a fifth order – the Composite – which combines features of the Corinthian with those of the Ionic. But Alberti was still perfectly objective and Vitruvian in his attitude. It was Sebastiano Serlio, nearly a century later, who really started the orders – the five orders now – on their long career of canonical, symbolic, almost legendary, authority. I am not sure that Serlio quite meant to do this but that is what he did.

Serlio was a man of the High Renaissance, an exact contemporary of Michelangelo, a near contemporary of Raphael and an associate of the architect-painter Baldassare Perruzzi whose designs he inherited. He built a few quite important buildings but his greatest service to architecture was to compile the first full-scale fully illustrated architectural grammar of the Renaissance. It came out as a series of books. The first two appeared in Venice, the later books in France under the patronage of François Ier. The books became the architectural bible of the civilized world. The Italians used them, the French owed nearly everything to Serlio and his books, the Germans and Flemings based their own books on his, the Elizabethans cribbed from him and Sir Christopher Wren was still finding Serlio invaluable when he built the Sheldonian at Oxford in 1663.

Serlio's book on the orders starts with an engraving – the very first of its kind (Plate 1) – in which all five orders are shown standing side by side like ill-assorted nine-pins ranged according to their relative slimness – that is to say according to the ratio of lower diameter to height. All are on pedestals. The stubby Tuscan is on the left; then the similar but slightly taller Doric; the elegant Ionic; the lofty, elaborate Corinthian; and finally the still more elongated and further enriched Composite. In the text accompanying this plate Serlio explains himself. He says that just as the ancient dramatists used to preface their plays with a prologue telling audiences what it was all going to be about, so he is putting before us the principal characters in his treatise on architecture. He does it in a way which makes the orders seem as categorical in the grammar of architecture as, say, the four conjugations of verbs in the grammar of the Latin language.

This very effective and, quite literally, dramatic gesture of Serlio's was not lost upon his successors, and the five orders as a 'complete set', all deviations from which were questionable, passed from hand to hand. Nearly all seventeenth and eighteenth century primers of architecture start in the same way, with a plate of the five columns and entablatures ranged side by side – Bloem in Switzerland, De Vries in Flanders, Dietterlin in Germany, Fréart and Perrault in France and, in England, Shute, Gibbs and Sir William Chambers. George Gwilt's edition of Chambers carries us up to 1825 and if you go from this to the same author's *Encyclopedia of Architecture* and follow this work to its latest edition in 1891 you will find it still being stated there that 'in the proper understanding and application of the orders is laid the foundation of architecture as an art'. As little as forty years ago when I was a student in the Bartlett School at University College, London, it was taken for granted that one's first task as a student was to draw out in great detail three of the classical orders.

Now there are two important points about all this. The first is to realize that although the Romans clearly accepted the individuality of Doric, Ionic and Corinthian, and knew about their historical origins, it was not they who embalmed and sanctified them in the arbitrary, limiting way with which we are familiar. The second point is to realize the immense importance, for the whole of architecture since the Renaissance, of this process of embalming, of canonization. The orders came to be regarded as the very touch-stone of architecture, as architectural instruments of the greatest possible subtlety, embodying all the ancient wisdom of mankind in the building art – almost, in fact as products of nature herself.

And this is where the modern eye must often confess itself defeated. Unless you really *know* your orders and can recognize, at a glance, a Tuscan according to Vitruvius, a Corinthian from the temple of Vespasian or an Ionic from the temple of Saturn or the rather odd Composite concocted by Serlio from the Colosseum you will not appreciate all the refinements and variations which, from time to time have been lovingly and assiduously applied to them. Nevertheless, even an 'O level' understanding of the orders is something, for it is by no means only in the handling of the orders themselves that the character of classical architecture lies. It is also – even more (much more, in fact) in the way they are deployed; but that is a subject for another talk.

Meanwhile, let us be quite clear about how variable or how invariable the orders are. Serlio puts them before us with a tremendous air of authority giving dimensions for each part as if to settle the profiles and proportions once and for all. But in fact, Serlio's orders, while obviously reflecting Vitruvius to some extent, are also based on his own observation of ancient monuments and thus, by a process of personal selection, to quite a considerable degree his own invention. It could hardly be otherwise. Vitruvius' descriptions have gaps in them and these can only be filled from knowledge of surviving Roman monuments themselves. The orders as exemplified in these monuments vary considerably from one to the other so it is open to anybody to abstract what he considers the best features of each in order to set out what he considers his ideal Corinthian, Ionic or whatever it is. All through the history of classical architecture speculation as to the ideal types of each of the orders has continued, oscillating between antiquarian reverence on the one hand

and sheer personal invention on the other. Somewhere between the extremes have been the types composed and published by the great theorists – Serlio, of course, first in 1537, then Vignola in 1562, Palladio in 1570 and Scamozzi in 1615. These have had a normalizing effect all over the world. But in all the centuries there have been instances where architects have taken pride in quite literally copying specific antique examples. For instance, Jean Bullant at Écouen, the great house near Paris, derived the Corinthian with most of its ornaments from the Temple of Castor and Pollux; that was in 1540. Inigo Jones at Covent Garden in 1630 reconstructed the Tuscan on the basis of Vitruvius' text (Plate 19) – almost an archaeological exercise. Then Sir John Soane in 1793 borrowed literally from the Temple of Vesta at Tivoli for the Bank of England. On the other hand, there have always been daring innovators. Philibert de L'Orme invented a new 'French' order for the Tuileries Palace; Wendel Dietterlin's orders in his book of 1594 are phantasmagoric variations on Serlio; Borromini's orders are outrageous and extremely expressive inventions, entirely his own. So it is a mistake ever to think of the 'five orders of architecture' as a sort of child's box of bricks which architects have used to save themselves the trouble of inventing. It is much better to think of them as grammatical expressions imposing a formidable discipline but a discipline within which personal sensibility always has a certain play – a discipline, moreover, which can sometimes be burst asunder by a flight of poetic genius.

Now, at this point I am going to ask you to look again at the Doric order in the drawing on the endpapers. Because I think it may still puzzle you that the entablature has so many curious bits and pieces, all with names but with no particular decorative or symbolic value that you can see. Why mutules? Why triglyphs and metopes? Why the taenia and those odd little tassels called guttae? You may well ask. And I can only give you a very general answer. It is quite certain that the Doric order derives its forms from a primitive type of timber construction. Vitruvius tells us as much. When you are looking at a Doric order executed in stone you are looking, in effect, at a carved representation of a Doric order constructed of wood. Not a literal representation, of course, but a sculptural equivalent. The earliest temples in the ancient world were of wood. Gradually some of these temples – those, doubtless of special sanctity and which attracted wealth – came to be rebuilt in stone. It would be felt imperative to preserve in the more permanent stone version the actual forms round which so much sanctity had gathered. Hence, the carpentry devices of the wooden entablature, already, no doubt, somewhat stylized, were copied in stone or marble. Later on, no doubt, stone temples on new sites copied the copies, and so it went on till the whole thing became a static and accepted formula.

Look at the Doric entablature again in the light of this and it does, to some extent, explain itself. The *mutules* seem to be the ends of cantilevers jutting out to support the eaves and to carry the eaves, from which the rain drips, well away from the columns. Then the *triglyphs* could be the ends of cross beams resting on the architrave. The *taenia* looks like some kind of binding member and it appears to be secured to the triglyphs by the *guttae*, which are not tassels, of course, but pegs. I say 'seem to be', 'could be', 'looks like' because all these things are my own rough guesses. Some archaeologists have devoted much ingenuity to trying to work

back from the formalized Doric to its last timber prototype. Their guesses are worth more than mine, but guesses they are and are likely to remain. All that matters for us now is that in the process of time a system of timber construction, copied in stone, crystallized into the linguistic formula which Vitruvius knew, and so we know, as the Doric order. This crystallization has a very obvious parallel in language. Words, expressions, grammatical constructions have all at some time had to be invented to meet particular needs of communication. Those immediate needs are long since forgotten, but the words and their patterns still form the language we use for a thousand purposes – including poetry. That is how it is with the five orders of architecture.

One more word about the orders. They are always supposed to have something resembling personalities; Vitruvius was perhaps responsible for this. The Doric he saw as exemplifying 'the proportion, strength and grace of a man's body' – presumably an average well-built male. The Ionic, for him, was characterized by 'feminine slenderness' and the Corinthian as imitating 'the slight figure of a girl', which may seem not very different from the last. But Vitruvius having opened the door to personalization of the orders the Renaissance let in a lot more – often very contradictory. Thus while Scamozzi echoes Vitruvius in calling the Corinthian 'virginal', Sir Henry Wotton, a few years later, distorts him by calling it 'lascivious' and 'decked like a wanton courtezan', adding that the morals of Corinth were bad anyway. Nevertheless, the Corinthian has always been regarded as female and the Doric as male, with the Ionic in between as something rather unsexed – an ageing scholar or a calm and gentle matron. Serlio's recommendations are perhaps the most specific and consistent. The Doric, he says, should be used for churches dedicated to the more extraverted male saints – St Paul, St Peter or St George and to militant types in general; the Ionic for matronly saints – neither too tough nor too tender and also for men of learning; the Corinthian for virgins, most especially the Virgin Mary. To the Composite Serlio awards no special characteristics, while the Tuscan he finds suitable for fortifications and prisons.

Now there is no need to take any of this too seriously. Certainly, there is no need when you are looking at the Corinthian columns of, say, the Mansion House in London, to wonder if the Lord Mayor who commissioned them thought of them as virginal or the other thing. The fact is that the orders have mostly been used according to taste, according to circumstances and very often according to means – building in plain Tuscan or Doric being obviously less expensive than building in richly carved Corinthian. There *are* cases where the use of an order has a deliberate symbolic significance. I think, for instance, that Wren must have used Doric at Chelsea Hospital because of its soldierly

character. And there is the fascinating case of Inigo Jones and the Tuscan at Covent Garden which I shall come to in another talk. Tuscan and Doric are the two most primitive orders and architects have tended to use them when they wanted to express roughness and toughness or in the case of the Doric what is called a 'soldierly bearing'. At the other end of the scale the Composite is sometimes quite obviously chosen because the architect wants to lay it on thick – luxury, opulence, no expense spared.

Anyway, the main point is this. The orders provided a sort of *gamut* of architectural character all the way from the rough and tough to the slim and fine. In true classical designing the selection of the order is a very vital point – it is a choice of mood. What you do with the order, what exact ratios you give its different parts, what enrichments you put in or leave out, this again shifts and defines the mood.

Well, so much for the Five Orders of Architecture – five basic elements in the architectural grammar of Antiquity. But what can you do with the orders? How does the grammar work? That I shall try to explain in my next talk.

2. The Grammar of Antiquity

So far, I have devoted nearly all my time to the Five Orders and I hope you are not tired of them because they are going to be with us more often than not. From now on, however,

I shall take your familiarity with them for granted and talk less about the orders themselves than about how they are used. Just look for the last time at Plate 1. These orders, what are they? They are columns supported on pedestals (whose use is optional) and carrying beams with projections to support the eaves of a roof. What can you do with them? Well, if you are designing a temple with porticos at front and back and colonnades at the sides, these columns and their appurtenances account for very nearly everything, so far as the exterior is concerned. At each of the four corners of the temple, the gable splits off from the cornice to form, front and back, that flat triangular shape which is called a pediment; and there you are. But suppose you are *not* designing a temple. Suppose you are designing a large and complicated structure like a theatre or courts of justice, a structure of several storeys involving arches and vaults and many windows and doors, what then? Common sense would suggest that you then scrap the orders as being irrevocably associated with temples and start all over again letting your arches and vaults and window-patterns find an expression of their own. That may be modern common sense but it is not what happened and it is not the view the Romans took when they adopted the arch and the vault for their public buildings. Far from leaving the orders out when they built vaulted amphi-theatres, basilicas and triumphal arches, they brought them in, in the most conspicuous way possible, as if they felt (which perhaps they did) that no building could communicate anything unless the orders were involved in it. To them the orders *were* architecture. Perhaps it was, in the first instance, a question of carrying over the prestige of temple architecture into great secular projects. I do not know. Anyway, the Romans took this highly stylized but structurally quite primitive kind of architecture and married it to arched and vaulted multi-storey buildings of great elaboration. And

in doing so they raised architectural language to a new level. They invented ways of using the orders not merely as ornamental enrichments for their new types of structure but as controls. The orders are, in many Roman buildings, quite useless structurally but they make their buildings expressive, they make them speak; they conduct the building, with sense and ceremony and often with great elegance, into the mind of the beholder. Visually, they dominate and control the buildings to which they are attached.

How is this done? Not just by pinning columns and entablatures and pediments on to an otherwise bare structure. The whole thing – structure and architectural expression – must be integrated, and this means that columns must be introduced in a variety of different ways. You see, there are columns and columns. Columns in the round have to carry something. Mostly they carry their own entablature and perhaps a wall or perhaps only the eaves of a roof above it. But you can have what are called 'detached columns' which have a wall behind them which they just do not touch but into which their entablature is firmly built. Then you can have three-quarter-columns, one quarter of each being buried in the wall. Similarly you can have half columns, half buried in the wall. And finally you can have 'pilasters' which are flat representations of columns, carved as it were in relief on the wall (or you can think of them, if you like, as built-in square columns). There you have four degrees of integration of an order in a structure – four degrees of relief, four strengths of shadow. The Romans never learnt to exploit the full possibilities of this, though they showed the way. To illustrate most forcibly what I have been saying I suggest you look at Plates 41, 42 and 43 – three church façades of the sixteenth-seventeenth centuries. The Gesù, Rome, is mostly pilasters. S. Susanna has pilasters above and pilasters, half-columns and three-quarter-columns below. The Val de Grâce in Paris has a porch with columns in the round, half-columns, three-quarter-columns and pilasters. I shall have more to say about these three buildings later on. Just now, I am trying to get your eye in to the kinds of play which become possible with the orders as a very long-term result of what the Romans pioneered. And while you are looking at these three churches note one other thing. Every time an order changes its plane of relief – say from pilaster forward to half, from half forward again to three-quarter, the entablature has to break forward too. You cannot dodge columns about under an unchanging entablature. That is one of the rules.

You will understand from all this, I think, just what I mean when I say that in the classical language the orders are not merely pinned on to the structure but integrated with it. Sometimes they sink right into it, sometimes they come walking out of it into a free-standing porch or colonnade. And all the time they *control* it.

Now back to ancient Rome. I emphasized earlier that all major Roman buildings other than temples were designed on the basis of arches and vaults, whereas the orders belong strictly to the more primitive system of 'trabeation' – that is to say, post and lintel construction. To marry the two in the sense of giving the old types of temple column the job of carrying arches could work up to a point but it was never satisfactory for two reasons. First because the columns and their entablatures had become so closely identified by long association as one thing, that to divorce them meant a sort of mutilation. Second because arched and vaulted buildings of any size require not columns but massive piers to take the loads. Columns are too slender. So what did the Romans do? The Colosseum at Rome answers the question at once. Plate 3 shows the least damaged side of that astonishing building. Here you see its three interminable open galleries – arch upon arch, with an additional solid storey at the top. And you see that every row of arches is framed inside a continuous colonnade. The colonnades have no structural purpose – or very little. They are representations of temple architecture carved, as it were, in relief on a building which is not a temple, which is multi-storeyed and is built as a system of arches and vaults.

If this way of combining the arcuated and trabeated systems – treating the trabeated system simply as a means of expression – seems to us absurdly simple, that is chiefly because we are so used to it. It *is* simple, but when you begin to examine it in detail, not as simple as all that. We have here in the Colosseum four orders – Doric on the ground floor, Ionic on the next, Corinthian on the uppermost open storey and on the plain storey above an indeterminate order (which has sometimes been called Composite but which is in fact unique to the Colosseum). Now focus on one bay of one of the open storeys – say of the middle storey which is Ionic. Plate 4 (immediately to the right of the Colosseum photograph) is a measured drawing of one such bay. Here you have a grammatical construction which is a pretty complete thing. It is controlled by an Ionic order which obeys nothing but its own traditional aesthetic rules. The shape and size of the piers behind the columns and of the arch, on the other hand, have come about through the exigencies of convenience and construction. The two disciplines have got to meet each other harmoniously and I think we may agree that they do. The pedestal moulding of the order ranges with the cill height of the arched gallery. The impost of the arch strikes the columns a little above half their height and the arch sits comfortably between the columns and the architrave above. If this arrangement is satisfactory it has been achieved by a very careful balancing of needs – the aesthetic dictatorship of the Ionic order and the practical needs of the building as a thing of use. A quite slight alteration to any part would wreck the whole thing. If for instance, you widened the opening by twelve inches, what would happen? The crown of the arch would go up by six inches. Assuming you want to keep the existing space between arch and entablature, the entablature would go up by six inches; so the columns would become six inches taller; and the rules of the Ionic order being what they are every other part of the order would have to be bigger. The pedestal would grow so its moulding would no longer range with the cill height and, worse still, the entablature, which you have already raised by six inches, would now grow in height and probably make trouble with the floor levels above, to say nothing of the proportions of the upstairs order, the Corinthian.

To be frank, I think this bay of the Colosseum is capable of a little more 'tolerance' than I have represented. But you will begin to see the kind of discipline which is involved in the classical language and which is inherent in it. And this discipline can be tightened. Look now at Plate 5. Here is the same arrangement, in principle, in a theoretical design by the sixteenth-century architect, Vignola. Vignola has obviously been determined to produce something in which all the parts are absolutely dependent on all the others. There is

no tolerance whatever round the arch. The piers are only just wide enough to receive the archivolt and the returns of the pedestal mouldings. The thing is as tight as a knot. If this design, as interpreted on your drawing-board, to your chosen scale, does not come naturally to terms with your planning and structural needs – well, you have got to play the game another way. And of course there are other ways, plenty, if you can think of them.

The Colosseum, which started us on this theme of arch and order in combination was, as you can imagine, one of the buildings from which the men of the Renaissance learnt most. It exemplifies not only this particular combination but also the superimposition of orders and, in the top storey, the use of a pilaster order to render expressive a plain, almost windowless wall. There were other buildings of this class – the theatre of Marcellus, for instance; and, outside Rome, the theatres at Verona and at Pola in Istria. All were closely studied, and useful grammatical elements extracted from them; they were published by Serlio and a generation later by Palladio. If you want to see Colosseum themes reflected in the works of Renaissance masters, here are three instances, more or less at random, among the illustrations. Plate 15: the Palazzo Corner, Venice, with its superimposed columns and arches. Plate 22: Mantua, where Giulio Romano romanticises the same theme. Or, for the pilastered upper storey of the Colosseum, Plate 31: the Castello Farnese at Caprarola. Very different buildings indeed but using those grammatical expressions of which the Colosseum was the most conspicuous exemplar.

Perhaps even more instructive, grammatically, than the theatres were the Triumphal Arches of Rome and other parts of Italy – Serlio gives as many as eleven. These arches, being purely ceremonial affairs, made great play with architectural and sculptural detail. In Rome, the largest and most important were and still are the Arch of Septimius Severus and the Arch of Constantine – the latter is illustrated in Plate 6. Now, look at this arch. What does it consist of? It is a massive rectangular slab of masonry with three holes in it – the centre hole is the main arch, the other two are lower and narrower subsidiary arches. Set against the four piers dividing the arches are four columns, standing on pedestals and rising to an entablature which breaks out over each separate column and at each of those points of breaking out carries a carved standing figure. Above the entablature is a superstructure called an attic storey. It makes a background for the figures and is carved in relief and lettered.

Now, observe the arrangement of all these elements. The keystone of the centre arch is hard up against the bottom of the entablature. The keystones of the side arches are hard up against a line which is that of the impost of the centre arch; and the three arches are all of the same ratio of height to width. The depth of the entablature is exactly such that the appropriate column, with its pedestal, fills the space between entablature and ground. An interesting, compact and harmonious arrangement admirably fulfilling its symbolic function. In the fifteenth century this arch and the other Roman arches had an enormous imaginative appeal both for painters and for architects (who, of course, often were painters) and, as a consequence, we find, over and over again, features and combinations of features which originated in the triumphal arches, being used in totally different sorts of buildings, all sorts of buildings, and used, once again, as grammatical ex-pressions controlling the structure.

By far the most impressive case of this is the conversion of the triumphal arch into a Christian church. This was achieved by Leon Battista Alberti. At Rimini, when he designed what we know as the Tempio Malatestiana, Alberti gave it a west front manifestly based on the Roman triumphal arch just outside the town. But that was only the first step. Much later, towards the end of his life, he designed the church of S. Andrea at Mantua and here he not only adapted the triumphal arch idea to the west front but brought it inside and made it the model for his nave arcades; and, more than that, he designed the west front and the arcades to the same scale, so that the whole church, inside and out, is, as it were, a logical three-dimensional extension of the triumphal arch idea. See Plates 7 and 8. I have deliberately kept the exterior (Plate 7) small because I much doubt Alberti's responsibility for some of its features – he died before it was built. But the main idea is clear enough and you will see how it is echoed again in the interior (Plate 8) – though here I must warn you against the frippery eighteenth-century wall decoration which in photographs always robs this building of much of its force. Here was a real triumph – at the same time a conquest of Roman grammar and the creation of a continuously logical structure on the model of which I do not know how many classical churches were to be built in the next four centuries. S. Andrea, Mantua, is the first great step towards St Peter, Rome, and St Paul, London.

There is much more I could say about triumphal arches and their contribution to the classical language. The most elementary fact of all about them – the division of a space by columns into three unequal parts: narrow, wide, narrow –

is perhaps also the most important. Plate 23 is a design for a gateway by Giulio Romano, obviously on the Triumphal Arch model. But to the left of this (Plate 22), and again on the opposite page (Plate 25), are buildings by the same artist in which the Triumphal Arch rhythm – narrow, wide, narrow – is also implicit. At a much later date, the attic storey was often found to be a useful element and a good background for figures. There is one at Somerset House (Plate 21) – though frankly I do not think it much helps the design in that instance. A really fine handling of an attic storey with figures is C. R. Cockerell's Ashmolean building at Oxford (Plate 35).

So now we have glanced at two types of Roman building – the galleried amphitheatre type, instanced by the Colosseum and the triumphal arch type – and seen the extent to which they were exploited as sources of grammatical expression. There are many other types of Roman architecture but none, I think, which were so completely digested and became so much an organic part of the classical language as these. There were the baths, of course, whose grandiose planning and vaulted halls and chambers became leading inspirations on certain occasions. There was the unique Pantheon, the prototype of all great classical domes; and the vast Basilica of Constantine, the challenge to all builders of great vaulted naves. And, of course, there were the temples. It is a curious fact that the typical Roman temple – the rectangular building with an open portico and pediment in front and with or without columns or pilasters all round (in fact, what we think of as the most obvious symbol of Roman architecture) was never used as a model for churches in Italy and never, indeed, in Europe till the eighteenth century. The circular temple, on the other hand, did play an important part. This was chiefly, perhaps, because of its very beautiful re-creation by Bramante, which I shall be describing later on.

But the great achievement of the Renaissance was not the strict imitation of Roman buildings (that was left for the eighteenth and nineteenth centuries) but the re-establishment of the grammar of antiquity as a universal discipline – *the* discipline, inherited from the remote past of mankind and applicable to all honourable building enterprises whatever. Of that grammar, that discipline, I have already perhaps said enough to convince you of its reality and also of its simplicity, but there is a little more you should know. There is, for instance, the very simple matter indeed of the spacing of columns – what is technically called 'intercolumniation'. Intercolumniation sets the 'tempo' of a building and once the tempo is set you cannot play fast and loose with it. Variations within the tempo – yes; but of specific and significant kinds.

The Romans attached so much importance to the spacing of columns that they established five standard types, measured in column diameters. Vitruvius records them. The closest spacing they called *Pycnostyle* – $1\frac{1}{2}$ diameters. Then came *Systyle*, *Eustyle*, *Diastyle* and finally the widest, *Araeostyle*, at 4 diameters. *Systyle* and *Eustyle* are the commonest. *Systyle* you might describe as a quick march, *Eustyle* as an easy dignified walk. The extreme intercolumniations neither march nor walk. *Pycnostyle* always seems to me to mean 'halt' – a palisade of men drawn up to attention. *Araeostyle* is a very long stride indeed, almost a slow leaping motion. If you like you can try to equate the intercolumniation with musical terminology. I would suggest, for *Diastyle*, 'adagio'; for *Eustyle*, 'andante' and for *Systyle*, 'allegro'; but I do not like 'presto' for *Pycnostyle*, still less 'largo' for *Araeostyle*. As with all analogies of this sort it is nonsense to press it too far. But the importance of intercolumniation – this system of 'beating time' in architecture – is, of course, immense. In Plates 10 and 11 there is a telling contrast which puts the whole thing in a nut-shell. Here are buildings of the same general shape and roughly the same commemorative purpose. But how different the emotions they arouse: Bramante's *Diastyle* (3 diameters) – stately, serene, meditative: Hawksmoor's *Pycnostyle* (1½ diameters) – tense and forbidding, a ceremonial palisade. And if you look through the other illustrations with this question of 'tempo' in mind you will be in no doubt about the importance of 'intercolumniation'. You will also begin to see the kind of variations which can be introduced – coupled columns, spaced pairs of columns, columns in the narrow-wide-narrow rhythm of the triumphal arch and the really intricate rhythms you get when columns, half columns and three-quarter columns begin to play together, sometimes (as in the church façades we looked at earlier on) leaving the basic tempo a matter of some doubt.

I have been talking all this time about grammar and about rules, to the extent that you may have begun to see the classical language as a frighteningly impersonal and intractable thing, something which challenges the architect at every turn, knocks his intuitions for six and allows him only a tiny margin of freedom in the choice of this rather than that. If you have received that impression I am not altogether sorry because that *is* part of the game. But there is something else – the architect's identification of himself with the very elements which defy him: so that he is intensely *with* the orders he is using as well as *up against* them, so that he almost believes himself to have designed the order whose manipulation gives him so many headaches. I cannot possibly illustrate this better than by quoting some remarks by a very great classical architect of the last generation – Sir Edwin Lutyens. Lutyens was brought up in the picturesque Tudor tradition of the late nineteenth century and to that tradition all his early houses belong. When he was thirty-five, however, in 1903, he began to have precisely those insights into the nature of classicism which were to make him eventually one of the architectural masters of his time. He was designing a house for a rich manufacturer at Ilkley when the splendour of the classical discipline seized him and in a letter to his friend Herbert Baker, he put down some wonderfully vivid flashes of thought:

> 'That time-worn doric order – a lovely thing – I have the cheek to adopt. You can't copy it. To be right you have to take it and design it. . . . You cannot copy: you find if you do you are caught, a mess remains.
>
> It means hard labour, hard thinking, over every line in all three dimensions and in every joint; and no stone can be allowed to slide. If you tackle it in this way, the Order belongs to you, and every stroke, being mentally handled, must become endowed with such poetry and artistry as God has given you. You alter one feature (which you have to, always), then every other feature has to sympathise and undergo some care and invention. Therefore it is no mean game, nor is it a game you can play lightheartedly.'

'You can't copy', says Lutyens. But on the other hand, in another letter:

'You cannot play originality with the Orders. They have to be so well digested that there is nothing but essence left. When right they are curiously lovely – unalterable as plant forms. . . . The perfection of the Order is far nearer nature than anything produced on impulse or accident-wise.'

There was an architect who really knew, because he learnt for himself, what the classical language meant. He loved, obeyed and defied the orders all at the same time. If the understanding of rule is one basic factor in the creation of great classical buildings the defiance of rule is the other. About that I shall have much to say later.

3. Sixteenth-Century Linguistics

I have been concerned with the grammatical workings of classical architecture – the mechanics of it: the nature of the Five Orders; columns, three-quarter and half columns; pilasters; the conjunction of columns with arches; intercolumniation, and all that. Now, getting a little warmer, I am going to talk about the handling of this grammar by some of the great innovating personalities of the sixteenth century and first of all by Donato Bramante.

The reason I go straight for Bramante is this. It was he, more than anybody else, who re-established the grammar of ancient Rome in buildings of pre-eminent consequence. I am not forgetting the performances of some of his prececessors: of Alberti, who, as we saw earlier, generated the perfect model for a classical church out of the Roman triumphal arch; of Brunelleschi, who earlier still, gave new breath to the Corinthian order in the naves of his Florentine churches. But it was Bramante who set the seal on all this,

who stated firmly and finally: 'this is the Roman language – this and no other is the way to use it'. Everybody recognized his authority. Serlio wrote that he was the man who revived the buried architecture of antiquity; and Serlio paid Bramante an even greater tribute when he included some of his works in the part of his book ostensibly devoted entirely to ancient Rome. For Serlio, Bramante was the exact equivalent of the antique.

Before Bramante came to Rome in 1499 he had worked in Milan in the court circle in which Leonardo da Vinci was the phenomenal presence. Leonardo was interested philosophically, diagrammatically, in architecture rather than in working it out in the orthodox forms of the antique. Bramante was interested in both, but more precisely in the working out and you can still see in Milan, tucked crookedly away off one of the busiest streets, his earliest work, the strange little church of S. Satiro, with its nave of piers, pilasters and arches and its choir which isn't there at all but is only represented in a marvellous perspective representation in low relief.

When Bramante came to Rome and entered the service of the Pope, he was already fifty-five and had only another sixteen years to live. But they were tremendously full years. Among other things he designed and partly built the new St Peter's and two great courts in the Vatican and if these talks were supposed to be a history of classical architecture I would have to settle down at this point to describing them. But I am quite content, for my present purpose, to take one building by Bramante and ask you to look at it rather closely. It is illustrated in Plate 10: the *tempietto* (little temple) in the cloister of S. Pietro in Montorio, Rome, built in 1502 on the traditional site of St Peter's martyrdom. This building is a reconstruction by Bramante of an ancient Roman circular temple – or so it seems at first. The picture to the left (Plate 9) is a real antique – the so-called temple of Vesta on the bank of the Tiber; it has lost the whole of its entablature and the rather pretty pan-tiled hat it wears is just a make-shift. But there (or in a temple of that sort) is Bramante's theme. He transposes it from Corinthian to Doric (Doric, perhaps, as appropriate to St Peter's militant sainthood). He mounts it on three steps and sets a continuous moulded plinth under the order. This plinth (which Serlio carelessly omitted in his engraving) gives the little building a sudden and auspicious 'lift' – enough to ratify its sanctity. Then comes the Doric order, then the balustrade. And each Doric column has an answering Doric pilaster (you can just see this in the photograph) on the wall of the inner building – what is called the *cella*. This cella rises higher than the colonnade and is covered

with a hemi-spherical dome. Now, is this a literal reconstruction of a Roman temple or is it not? Clearly not. It is an *extension* of an idea borrowed from the Romans. The plinth and the vertical penetration of the central cylinder up and through to a hemi-spherical dome are Bramante's inventions and highly successful ones to judge by the number of times they have been imitated.

This tempietto is a perfect piece of architectural prose – a statement, clear as a bell. Through Serlio's regrettably inaccurate engraving and, later, Palladio's more accurate one, the building became world-famous – as famous almost as the Pantheon or the Arch of Constantine and as much a 'classic'. Sir Christopher Wren knew it of course, through Palladio, and at one phase in the designing of St Paul's he tried using two Bramante temples as the top stages of his two western towers. That was while he was still struggling with all sorts of unmanageable alternatives for the great drum and dome over the Cathedral's transeptal space. Eventually it dawned on him that the *tempietto* was the clue to that problem even more than to the other, in spite of the enormous difference in size and site. Look at St Paul's dome (Plate 13) and you will see at once just how much it owes to the *tempietto*. But the more you look the more you will see that St Paul's dome is no mere enlargement of the *tempietto*. The *tempietto* has 16 columns – Wren required twice as many. A ring of 32 columns, Wren saw, would lack stable orientation; so he filled up every fourth intercolumniation – those which come over the great piers – and carved a niche in each, thus giving his colonnade a definite 'tempo' of four to the bar. So Wren's dome is no mere enlargement of Bramante but an imaginative extension – just as Bramante was an extension of the antique.

Over and over again, in the seventeenth and eighteenth centuries, this *tempietto* idea comes into play – the colonnade surrounding the cylindrical, domed core. Hawksmoor, in his mausoleum at Castle Howard (Plate 11) makes it tragic – columns close and forbidding like a palisade, dome deflated, un-aspiring; and for base a funereal platform, prostrating itself along the ground. But then look at the next picture (Plate 12), James Gibbs's Radcliffe library at Oxford. *Is* this the same theme? It is. But the columns have re-grouped themselves in pairs, pairs *un*equally spaced, over a podium which with its pedimented projections accents one set of intervals and under a dome whose buttresses descend emphatically over the other set. Curiously elaborate and sophisticated, it would have delighted a Gonzaga or a Medici and is perhaps slightly absurd for a building whose sole function is to make space for serious books and serious readers in an English university.

Plate 14 shows you another classic invention of Bramante's. It is the palace in Rome which Raphael, the painter, lived in for a time so that it is always called after him. It no longer stands. The main rooms of this palace were at the top. Below was a series of arches let off as shops – a common Roman practice. Bramante has given the lower part the rough but disciplined character of Roman engineering works. To the upper part only he has attached an order – Doric, coupled, on pedestals, the pedestals ranging with the balustrades of the windows. Elementary it may seem to us – a direct prose statement. But, as in the case of the *tempietto* it was new. The Romans had not done this – not quite. It was, once again, an extension of Rome, appropriate to six-teenth-century life. And, once again, this new classic echoes down the centuries to our own. Sansovino brought it to Venice (Plate 15) and the Grand Canal. They do not have shops on the Grand Canal; so here the three middle arches of the ground floor become a grand entrance while the side arches are replaced by windows. And, Venice demanding additional height, Sansovino duplicated Bramante's upper storey, arriving at something which faintly but I think deliberately echoes the Roman Colosseum. Then, nearer home, if you turn to Plate 21, there is the Strand front of Somerset House, a clear descendant of Bramante: date, 1780. And when you are in the Strand, just look across from there to the shop-filled arches and arrogantly bedizened Doric columns of Australia House – Bramante again, in the age of British Imperialism: date, 1911.

Bramante led architecture in Italy to that stage of complete conquest of the antique and complete confidence in extending and adapting it which we call, in all the arts, the High Renaissance. The generation which followed and accepted him included Raphael, the painter who was also on occasion an architect; Baldassare Peruzzi; the younger Antonio da Sangallo; Sansovino who, as we have seen, brought Bramante's (and incidentally Peruzzi's) ideas to Venice; and Sammichele who took them to and developed them in Verona. But on none of these names am I going to dwell; if I did it would be a question mostly of trying to define what they owed to Bramante and in what special directions each of them departed. Instead, I want to move on to the next generation after that and talk of Palladio – Andrea Palladio; because we are thinking about Architecture as a language and from this point of view it is more rewarding to put Palladio next to Bramante, even though Bramante died three years before Palladio was born. From Bramante to Palladio is an easy step and this is why. Palladio, a miller's son, came up out of obscurity and spent most of his life in a rather obscure little north-Italian town called Vicenza. There, he grew up among a small land-owning intelligentsia to whom Rome was a very long way off indeed. They had, as it were, their own belated High Renaissance. When Palladio got to Rome as a young man the first thing which must have struck him was the appalling inadequacy of the only published drawings of the Roman ruins – those of our old friend Serlio, whose book was then fairly new. Palladio would feel that Serlio had only scratched the surface of these studies, had omitted much that was valuable and had never really much conception of those refinements of profile and proportion which were the essence of the antique. So Palladio became a scholar of architecture, the most learned and exact of his time. But he became much more than that. He overtook Bramante's mastery of the grammar of Roman architecture and when opportunities came to him – as they did, thick and fast, in and around Vicenza and later in Venice – he built buildings in which the language of Rome was more eloquent, more articulate, than it had ever been.

When I say 'more articulate', I mean something quite precise. Let me demonstrate. Look back, first, to Plate 8, the photograph of the interior of S. Andrea, Mantua; and then turn forward to Plate 17, the photograph of the interior of Il Redentore, Venice. There is almost exactly a hundred years between the building of these two churches, the first by Alberti, the second by Palladio. You will see that the bay design – that is to say, the repeating unit of piers and arches –

is very much the same in both. But Alberti expresses himself only in pilasters, Palladio in half-columns. This is what I mean by articulation. In Palladio's church you are much more aware of the order than in Alberti's; and at the east end of the Redentore, Palladio's order becomes perfectly free as it turns round to form an apsidal screen behind the altar. It seems as if Palladio's church *really* is an affair of lofty columns supporting their heavy entablatures: the walls and arches seem merely to fill in between them.

Now look at Plate 16, Palladio's Chiericati Palace at Vicenza – an important town house in which the ground floor offers an open colonnade to the public and the first floor has two open balconies so that the walls only come out to the street front where they enclose the grand saloon in the centre. Again, Palladio makes his orders the dominant factor in the building. In both these buildings – in nearly all Palladio's buildings – you have the sense of his deep love of the orders and his great pride in exhibiting them in his own perfectionist versions. He was resurrecting Rome in Vicenza and the Veneto with even more realism than Bramante had resurrected it in Rome herself.

Now this realism in recalling Rome is only one aspect of Palladio. It happens to be the one that best suits my exposition at the moment. And it is, of course, inseparable from another aspect I have already mentioned – Palladio the archaeologist. Archaeologist is perhaps not quite the right word because Palladio's enquiries into the past were more strongly tinged with imaginative awareness of what might have been than we should think quite proper. Still, call it archaeology. When Palladio investigated the text of Vitruvius or the ruins of Rome his results led him at once to make 'restorations' and these restorations were among the most exciting things in his book – or rather books: I mean the four books (the *Quattro Libri*), published in 1570. The effect of these reconstructions reached far beyond Italy: in fact they were more fertile outside Italy than in and their impact in England was rather specially important. In Plate 19 you see the portico of St Paul's Covent Garden. This is by Inigo Jones but it is based on Palladian archaeology. It follows (though with certain expert and sensitive deviations) Palladio's literal interpretation of what Vitruvius tells us about the Tuscan order. Those fine, spreading eaves, those wide-apart columns, are Palladian archaeology.

A hundred years after Inigo Jones, Lord Burlington availed himself of Palladio's archaeology when he built the Assembly Rooms at York. Plates 18 and 20 show just how literally he did so. But this building has significance in another context and I shall return to it later on.

Now in taking Bramante and certain aspects of Palladio together I have been confining myself to the grand simplicities of sixteenth-century Italy – the re-establishment of the Latin of architecture: the orders arrogantly displayed and drilled with absolute conviction. It is just possible, I think, that along with the completeness, the authority, the finality of all this you may have begun to feel a certain uneasiness – not to say boredom. The five orders can, of course, become the most terrific bore. If you do feel a slight uneasiness you are not alone – you are very much with some of the more adventurous and romantic personalities of the generation which followed Bramante; some of the men who were in Rome when he died in 1515, who were still in Rome when Raphael died in 1520 and perhaps still about the place when

it was sacked and pillaged by the Imperial troops in 1527. There was at that time a very considerable uneasiness about what the High Renaissance (as we call it now) had achieved. There are signs of an incipient malaise even in some of Raphael's last works and in the work of one of his pupils, Giulio Romano, there is positive revolt – a romantic dash for freedom.

But I cannot begin to talk about Giulio without explaining the meaning of a word of great significance in classical architecture from this time on – *rustication*. What is rustication? As the word rather implies, it was at fir t conceived to mean a rough countrified way of laying stones, each particular stone retaining some of the individuality it had when hewn from the quarry. However, this rustic roughness was recognized as having character – artistic possibilities – and it became in due course the subject of extreme sophistication. Already, by the time Serlio was writing his fourth book (published 1537) rustication had been stylised and systematised, as you can see by his engraving, reproduced in Plate 24. From being just rough it had become highly artificial – cut into geometrical facets. Serlio describes rustication, however, as being fundamentally a mixture of the natural and the artificial – he seems to imply a sort of struggle between the artificer and the forces of nature. This, of course, is a thoroughly romantic idea and in the works of Giulio Romano we can see it at work. Look at the detail, Plate 25, of the Palazzo del Tè – the summer palace of the Dukes of Mantua. Here is a very strange performance. You recognize, of course, the Doric order. And the major columns are approximately on the triumphal-arch pattern. But while the outside columns have plinths to themselves, the inner columns share their plinths, most illogically, with an intrusive minor Doric which frames the arch. Everything is a bit uneasy, a bit wrong. Do you notice that in the entablature some of the stones have slipped? And do you notice that these 'slipped' stones occur in exactly the same places on either side of the centre?

What is this all about? That it represents a flight from everything Bramante stood for is pretty obvious. It is irrational, impressionistic. It recalls ruins (especially, of course, in the deliberately dropped stones). It recalls ancient buildings left half-finished. But it has great power and this is very largely because of the dramatic use of rustication. The stones seem to be quarrelling all the time with the highly finished architectural detail. The rough key-stones in the two side recesses are forcing a cornice up into the stones above. The key-stones of the two round-headed niches are grotesquely too big, that of the centre arch is absurdly small. In patches, here and there, there is no rustication at all and suddenly the wall looks embarrassingly naked.

How serious is all this? Well, I am sure it is not meant to be funny. It is an arrogant protest against rules and – yes, it is poetry; a poetry which has something to do with grottos and with the cult of giants and dwarfs which seems to have haunted the court of Federigo Gonzaga. For us now, the importance of it all is the quantity of sheer invention it contains. Giulio didn't invent rustication (the Romans used it; Brunelleschi used it; Bramante had used it in the House of Raphael), but Giulio did bring it to a pitch of expressiveness which no one else had dreamed of and from which very few architects after his time failed to benefit. From the Palazzo del Tè, he went on to the Ducal Palace itself and built that unforgettable study in the classical-grotesque which you see in Plate 22 – the Cortile della Cavallerizza. And lastly, to complete our glimpse of Giulio look at his design (Plate 23) for a city gateway – a triumphal arch conceived entirely in terms of this same exaggerated toughness.

The long-term effect of Giulio's inventions was tremendous. Even Palladio, who you might think, from what I have said of him, would be proof against such explosive stuff, borrowed from him in his later palaces. In eighteenth century England, Newgate Prison (which you see in Plate 50) had Giulio to thank for its horrific solemnity. And you cannot walk through any commercial centre built up in the nineteenth-twentieth centuries without seeing Banks and Insurance Offices loaded up with rustic devices, many of which have their origin in Mantua. Look at the load carried by London's elected representatives at County Hall (Plate 51).

But I must end up by introducing you to a much greater revolutionary than Giulio Romano, to the man who really did outrage the authority of the High Renaissance and turn classical architecture into new courses – Michelangelo.

Michelangelo was twenty-five years older than Giulio Romano, but had done no architecture at all when Giulio began the Palazzo del Tè; and his major works nearly all belong to the period after Giulio's death in 1546 when he himself was over seventy. His architecture is a world away from Giulio's. Rustication had almost no interest for him. His walls are smooth and their power is concentrated into tightly bounded surfaces, recessions and projections and moulded elements which are rarely enriched. Michelangelo always insisted that he was not an architect but a sculptor yet no professed architect has ever had so startling an effect on architecture. Vasari said of him that 'he broke the bonds and chains of a way of working that had become habitual by common usage'. That is, if anything, an understatement; it does scant justice to the positive effects of Michelangelo's inventions, the enormous incentive they supplied.

The 'way of working' mentioned by Vasari was, of course, the way of the High Renaissance masters since Bramante – that is to say, the grammatical approach through a study of Vitruvius, filled out by prolonged observation of the antiquities of Rome – we had all that in my second talk. Cornice profiles and the dressings of doors and windows were all designed with reference to antique authority. If an architect's own sensitivity entered into his designs it was involuntary and through chinks in the process of selection from the consecrated sources. Now, on this whole idea of 'authority' Michelangelo turned his back. He was already a sculptor with a mastery of form and material transcending the antique and when he turned to architecture this same power of seeing through the dead, accepted forms to something intensely alive, enabled him to transcend, with absolute assurance, the Vitruvian grammar. As Vasari says, rather naively, 'he proceeded quite differently in proportion, composition and rules from what others had done fo lowing common practice'. He did indeed – quite differently.

Look at Plates 26 and 27. Here are two architectural frames or 'aedicules' by two great classical masters. The one on the left is by Raphael, a beautifully elegant piece of classical prose at the Palazzo Pandolfini, Florence. Perfect of its kind, but not exactly moving; and nearly every line can be described categorically in Vitruvian terms. On the right is an aedicule by Michelangelo – one of the niche-like recesses in the Medici Chapel at S. Lorenzo. This is almost impossible to describe in words. It has – just to say – some of the main elements of the Raphael work: pilasters, pediment, architrave but all are re-invented and full of what a Vitruvian critic would have to call gross and absurd errors. Are the pilasters Doric, or what? What is the sense of those breaks in the curved line of the pediment? And by what rule or precedent does an architrave moulding go sliding up into the tympanum to lean its sharp elbows on a cornice? No, this work is really almost abstract sculpture. It is Michelangelo's personal equivalent of the Vitruvian. It strikes the beholder, perhaps, as strange, even at first unacceptable. But it stays in the memory, this curiously tense, deeply felt creation. No architect – anyway no young and impressionable architect – who visited the Medici chapel when Michelangelo had done with it could ever feel quite the same about architecture again.

4. The Rhetoric of the Baroque

I ended my last talk by saying that no architect – anyway no young and impressionable architect – who visited the Medici Chapel at Florence, when Michelangelo had done with it, could ever feel quite the same about architecture again. Why not? Well, I do not know. I can only leave those two illustrations – Plates 26 and 27 – to speak for themselves. I suppose it is necessary to feel the conventionality of the Raphael aedicule (on the left) in order to feel the startling unconventionality of the Michelangelo aedicule (on the right). Michelangelo's distortions of the Latin of architecture here are rather like his distortions of the human body in many of his sculptures; only we all know, or think we know, the human body and easily grasp the significance of distortions, while few of us know our architectural Latin very well. Anyway, I think that someting of the intensity of Michelangelo's handling of architectural form is inescapable; it does not surely have to be underlined by comparisons and analogies.

Michelangelo's other architectural works have not all this same intense originality of detail – they surprise us in other ways. Look at Plate 28, one of the palaces on the Capitoline Hill at Rome. Here Michelangelo is using a very big and quite conventional Corinthian pilaster order. But there are two special things about it. One is that it *is* very big – the pilasters are forty-five feet high and so are going in the direction of Michelangelo's St Peter's where they become simply colossal – in fact ninety feet high. The other thing is that these pilasters pass through two storeys. The Romans had never done this: in fact the Capitoline palaces are, very roughly, like Roman temples whose sides have been 'filled in', with modern work – walls and windows above, an open storey below. And notice that the upper wall rests on an entablature supported by Ionic columns – two to a bay. This arrangement, this way of making two orders work together to control a two-storey building – was one of Michelangelo's most valuable and liberating inventions.

It is an easy step from the Capitoline palace to the two church façades illustrated on the same page. Both of them (most obviously S. Andrea al Quirinale on the left) make use of the Capitoline theme. But these churches are more than a hundred years later than the Capitoline. They are what is called Baroque and I cannot talk about Baroque without first trying to give you some idea what went on in Italian architecture between the time that the double impact of Giulio Romano and Michelangelo was first received in the 1530s and 1540s and the time when the Baroque got into its stride a century later.

There is a name for what went on and it is 'Mannerism'. Mannerism means very much what we mean when we talk of a person being 'mannered' – that is to say, affecting to imitate a type and in doing so showing an artificiality, an affectation of manner. Mannerism is not a style. It is the 'mood' of an age and all sorts of very different things happened while that mood prevailed. For our purpose, which is to consider architecture as a language, what we want to know is the extent to which Mannerism coloured the language and enriched its vocabulary. In Plates 31 and 41 are two very famous buildings by Vignola, both of which are always considered outstanding monuments of the age of Mannerism. Take first Plate 31 – the Castello Farnese, Caprarola. I must explain at once that the bastion-like features at the corners of the house are the result of the foundations having been laid and the walls partly carried up on another plan by another architect. Apart from these, the main block of the house could be, for all you can see in the photograph, simply an extension of High Renaissance practice – something that Bramante perhaps and Raphael certainly might have composed – though a rather obvious divergence is that the three-arched loggia between the curving steps is rusticated (rather gently) in the manner of Giulio Romano.

But now look at the engraving (Plate 34) on the opposite page, from Vignola's book. This is a detail of the main entablature at Caprarola. It is not quite like any of the entablatures in our Plates 1 and 2 though it has something in common with Serlio's rather ugly version of the Composite and this in fact is the clue. Serlio's source for his Composite was the pilastered top storey of the Colosseum (Plate 3 if you want to check your memory): the top storey at Caprarola, with its pilasters, is based on this same theme. But Vignola has very brilliantly invented an entablature which is, at one and the same time, nicely in scale with the pilaster order below it and big and bold enough to form a crowning feature for the whole mass of the building. It is a departure from the strict grammar of the antique – a departure in the direction of inventive modelling, of designing a façade as a pattern in light and shade, a pattern through which runs a

play of meaning rather than any precise series of statements.

This way of putting it may be clearer when applied to a more thoroughly Mannerist façade; so turn to the second Vignola building I mentioned – the church of the Gesù, the principal church of the Jesuit order in Rome (Plate 41). This is a huge church (photographs always make it look too small) with a huge west front in two pilastered storeys, both of them Corinthian. If you look at this building carefully and try to spell out its architecture in High Renaissance terms you soon get into difficulties. There is no clear repetitive rhythm. Surfaces advance and recede in a baffling way and at one point on the ground storey, one pilaster seems to be partly tucked in behind another. Obviously the whole thing is meant to be received as a broad piece of architectural modelling within which, as I said before, a certain play of meaning resides.

It is important to understand these products of the age of Mannerism because their effect reached a very long way. The early Victorians, for instance, re-discovered Mannerist architecture (though they did not call it that – they just called it Italian). They rediscovered Mannerist architecture as something exactly suited to themselves. It seemed to release them from the cold pedantry of the classical revivals and it had what they liked to call 'character'. Most of the big, black banks and many of the more ornate warehouses in places like Manchester, Liverpool and Leeds are thoroughly 'Mannerist' in inspiration and most of them are terrible rubbish, interesting now only because for us they reflect the Victorian image so sharply. But occasionally the artistry of the original Mannerists shines through as it does in the work of our one Victorian classical architect of international calibre, Charles

Robert Cockerell. The little drawing, Plate 32, shows how Cockerell drew from Caprarola most of what he needed for an insurance office in the city of London. The photograph to the right of it, Plate 33, is to show, in parenthesis, what somebody else made of Cockerell fifty years later – a regular fruit-salad of Mannerist *and* Baroque material, a piece of professional showmanship exactly suited to the mood of *fin-de-siécle* critics who, for a few years, thought the Chartered Accountants Institute the most wonderful modern building in London.

Cockerell is worth much more attention than this kind of thing and for sheer wit and invention in the handling of Mannerist themes there is no building in Britain quite like his Ashmolean building in Oxford (Plate 35). Cockerell saw with the eyes of the Italian mannerists but saw far more; and the Greek detail of which, as an archaeologist, he was a master, wonderfully enriches the Mannerist idiom of Vignola, whose famous cornice – re-profiled – you will at once recognize.

In our next five plates (36–40), Mannerism is shown penetrating in another direction altogether. On the extreme left (Plate 36) we have a charming work by the Florentine Mannerist architect (who was also a sculptor), Ammanati – very tight and tense with any amount of 'modelling' – sunk panels raised panels, raised panels within sunk panels and over the haunches of the arch on the ground floor a deliberate absurdity – two Ionic capitals carved as if in suspension, or as if they were part of a thin film of architecture partly cut away to reveal the arch. This sculptural attitude to façades, which derives ultimately from Michelangelo, is reflected again (but perhaps even more so) in Plate 37, the courtyard of the Palazzo Marino, Milan. This is a little square court-yard – three arches to each side –which few visitors to Milan ever bother to look at, though it is plumb in the centre of the City. The curious thing about this – a work of Galeazzo Alessi – is that, above the Doric order on the ground floor, with its very much contracted entablature, nearly everything has got turned into sculpture – or, rather, the architecture is put in in outline and the surfaces are filled with figure-sculpture, animal masks, swags and festoons of fruit and flowers. Instead of an upper order there are 'terms' – pedestals narrow at the base and widening to human busts at the top; between these 'terms' are niches containing figures; between the arches are elaborate panels containing sculpture in relief; and so on. All very theatrical and probably, indeed, of theatrical origin. Now this kind of architectural décor travelled very easily – anyway it travelled north very easily; furthermore it lent itself to the making of highly attractive engraved plates such as you see reproduced in Plates 38 and 39. These are by the Fleming, Vredeman de Vries, and the German, Wendel Dietterlin, respectively and they show the form in which the architecture of Mannerism reached – among other places – Elizabethan England. In fact, Wollaton Hall, on the right, is decorated very largely with quotations from De Vries. And although Dietterlin's frightfully intricate designs were not often copied in England, his book was so well known that Elizabethan and Jacobean ornament became generically known, in the seventeenth and eighteenth centuries as 'ditterling' ornament.

All this is taking us to the far outside edge of our subject and I am not inviting you for one moment to consider Wollaton Hall as an important manifestation of the classical language; it may be important for a great deal else, but not for that. To copy De Vries was to copy quite pretty paper patterns containing only a skin-deep appreciation of the kind of classical designing which these talks are about.

So let us get back to the centre of the stage. Plate 41 is the west front of the Gesù. On the same page are two other west fronts quite obviously deriving from it. Below is S. Susanna, Rome, and if you compare this with the Gesù you will be struck at once by two things. First, that it is much more compact; it insists definitely on a vertical rectangle and the scrolls over the aisles, which swing out in the Gesù, are here drawn firmly in to help the vertical stress. Second, you will feel, I think, that whereas the pattern of pilasters in the Gesù façade is diffuse, in S. Susanna the arrangement of columns and pilasters is unmistakeably designed to bring your attention to the centre and indeed to the central door. Now this comparison has often been made and is as handy a comparison as any to explain the difference between Mannerist and Baroque architecture – Santa Susanna is Baroque. But just to show how careful you have to be with these terms, look now at the third church on this page – the Val de Grâce, built in Paris fifty years later than S. Susanna. Mannerist? Baroque? Well, let us see. It has not the diffuseness and ambiguity of the Gesù; but neither has it the force and decision of S. Susanna. Nor is it merely something between the two. It has a character of its own. It is relaxed and harmonious and the gradual articulation of the ground floor order from pilaster to column-in-the-round seems to breathe a truer classical spirit than anything in the other two buildings. Mannerist? Baroque? No; neither. It is a personal interpretation, by a Frenchman, of the Gesù theme – and the interpretation belongs to a phase in French art which has classical standards of its own, the standards of Poussin, of Racine – and of Mansart, the architect of this church.

It is impossible to dodge the occasional embarrassment of these generalizing expressions – 'High Renaissance', 'Mannerist', 'Baroque', and so on. We cannot escape using them and in fact I have used one for the title of this talk, in calling it 'The Rhetoric of the Baroque'. Baroque is nearly always rhetorical, in the sense of grandiloquent, contrived, persuasive oratory; and if we are talking about architecture as a sort of language, this is a useful qualification of some of the greater buildings of the seventeenth century – the ones we mostly have in mind when we use the word 'Baroque'. And I am going to conclude this talk by considering three such works. First, the Piazza of St Peter's, Rome, by Bernini. Second, the east front of the Palais du Louvre, Paris, by Le Vau, Perrault and Le Brun. Third, Blenheim Palace, near Oxford, by Vanbrugh and Hawksmoor. In case anybody should want to ask me: 'are you quite sure all these are pure Baroque?' let me say at once that the answer is 'no, of course I am not sure'. For one thing there is no such category as 'pure Baroque' – just because there is a word, it does not mean there is a pure essence to match it. For another thing, while it could certainly be proved beyond reasonable doubt that these three buildings are entitled to the appellation Baroque, it could be shown with equal certainty that there are things about each which might *dis*qualify them in some contexts. So let us not bother. Let us just look at the buildings themselves and see what they have to say to us.

Bernini designed the piazza before St Peter's as a huge enclosed forecourt. As such you see it in the air-view, Plate

44, taken before the demolitions of Mussolini's time. It is a forecourt, not an 'approach': a forecourt, an enclosed space, an atrium, built with the specific purpose of accommodating great gatherings to receive the blessing of the Pope. Apart from the two straight corridors attaching themselves to the façade of the church, it consists of one immense oval space partly defined by two curved regiments of columns – columns fifty feet high and standing four deep. There are here in all 280 free-standing, fifty-foot high columns – probably the most imposing assembly of columns in the world. And the columns (some are shown in Plate 46, on the right), the columns are – what? Doric? Well, yes; except that they have Tuscan bases and are a trifle taller than the conventional Doric and that they carry an entablature which is not Doric at all but more or less Ionic. In other words, for this particular occasion, Bernini has taken the law into his own hands and designed his own order – an order fusing the soldierly dignity of the Doric with the elegance of the Ionic. It is a curiously memorable order. One remembers it, inevitably, as Doric (because of the capitals); but as a Doric with a personality entirely its own.

I want to make it clear what a tremendous impression these colonnades make. When you look at the photograph (Plate 46) remember that the columns are repeated three times behind what you see there, so that when you are inside the colonnades, on the route taken sometimes by great processions, these ascending cylinders press round you like forest trees. The sun strikes through as it may; and from this ceremonious forest you look across the Piazza to another, as large and as deep. Then notice how each of those two giant crescents, whose own rhythm could so easily run away with

them, are steadied by columns standing out at the ends and again, in coupled pairs, at the centre – sentinels. It is a marvellous performance and of course the opportunity was marvellous – and unique: the opportunity to build a structure of this size and to build it entirely of columns. The opportunity has, so far as I know, never occurred again – it has only been envied.

Now a Palace is a very different thing and when we turn to the Louvre in Paris (Plate 42) we do indeed see another colonnade but one whose existence has had to be contrived as part of a royal residence. The designing of this east front was one of the great episodes of European architectural history. The rest of the Louvre had been built, over a period of a hundred years and Colbert, Louis XIV's minister, was determined that the east front should be the culminating success of the whole. All the leading French architects were asked for designs and some famous Italians, too – including Bernini who visited Paris in great state and whose design was accepted. But it was not built. In the end, the work was entrusted to three men: Le Vau, the King's First Architect; Le Brun, his First Painter; and a physician of wide scientific attainments, Claude Perrault – and it is always supposed that Perrault's was the most original and innovating mind of the three.

The result is spectacular. Never had any Italian master succeeded – or perhaps ever had occasion to seek success – in the exposition of Roman temple architecture on this scale in combination with the purposes of a palace. But the first thing that strikes one about the Louvre is, of course, this Corinthian colonnade of fully articulated Roman columns. The columns are in pairs. We have seen this arrangement

31

before, in Bramante's house of Raphael (Plate 14); it is a good way of securing the wide intercolumniation you need for windows. But Bramante's columns were against a wall. At the Louvre the inner wall is, for part of the way, set right back so that the columns stand out as if they were indeed part of a temple colonnade. But taking the whole length of this façade together, you will see that, although the colonnade is an immediately striking and dramatic element in it, it is not the only factor which makes for its success. This is due to the handling of the order as a whole – its integration with the building, its control of the building. And how is this managed? In two long stretches, as we have just seen, the order has its independence. In the centre feature, however, it comes a pace forward and carries a pediment; and here the columns are backed by a solid wall – a wall, incidentally, which has an arch in it, covering the main entrance, and which (above the arch) is splendidly decorated with low-relief sculpture. Then in the end blocks (pavilions the French call them and so, mostly, do we) – in the end pavilions, the wall comes further forward and the order, with the same intercolumniation as in the colonnade, turns itself into pilasters. But in compensation, as it were, in the (subtly widened) middle intercolumniation in these end pavilions is a recess where the wall goes back to the plane of the wall in the centre pavilion, and moreover contains a round-arched window echoing the entrance arch in the centre. Follow this carefully in the illustration, because the Louvre is a wonderful example of the 'play' of a classical order in controlling a very long frontage not merely without monotony but with wit and grace and aesthetic logic. I will only add, concerning the Louvre, that the carved ornaments have crispness and

delicacy of a kind which is peculiarly French and which accounts for the extraordinary vitality of this building, which on a brilliant spring morning looks like the newest, freshest thing you ever saw in your life.

And now, lastly, another palace, but utterly different from the Louvre – Blenheim Palace (Plate 48). Not, this time, one long façade with subtle variations of plane but a building of many parts – deploying this way and that, advancing, receding; not one long serene sky-line but a silhouette in violent motion. Blenheim Palace, built by Queen Anne for the Duke of Marlborough as a reward for his services to the nation and at the same time as a monument to British military glory, was the joint work of Vanbrugh and Hawksmoor. It is easily one of the most complex classical buildings in all Europe. Why it is so complex I could only explain by going at length into Vanbrugh's ideas about architecture. There is not time for that and all I will say is that Vanbrugh fused in his work two very different influences. One was what you would expect – a passionate love of Roman architecture and all that the great masters and theorists had done with it (in that, he had the fullest possible support from his colleague, Hawksmoor). The other influence was an unexpected one for his time: Vanbrugh had a strong feeling for medieval castles and for those most daring of all English buildings, the great towered and turreted houses of Elizabethan and Jacobean times. At Blenheim these two influences merge in the exciting and apparently chaotic result you see. But Blenheim is not chaotic: it is most beautifully and logically put together, as perhaps I can show you even on the basis of the one small engraving before us.

Take first those two towers, left and right, heavily rusticated and crowned by a mass of piers and pinnacles. There are in fact four of these towers, though you can only see two clearly; and those four mark the four corners of a rectangle: they pin Blenheim down to the soil. These towers have no classical order. The rest of the house has – it is controlled by two orders: a fifty-foot Corinthian and a Doric half that height, and those two orders play a sort of counterpoint between, into and out from the towers. The centre block of the house is Corinthian – fully articulated columns in the portico, pilasters on either flank. The Doric order is, as it were, hiding in this block – it is just detectable in the sides of the ground floor windows: three each side of the portico. But in the wings, out it comes. There is a double beat, then it wheels round. Another double beat: it turns, enters the towers – it disappears. Then out it marches from the near side of each tower, marches forward till it is returned as a formal entry with steps inside and a flourish of arms above. That is very roughly the lay-out of this architectural manoeuvre – this still choreography. There is a great deal more to Blenheim than that. There is the way the verticals of the portico shoot up through the pediment and then run back to meet the gable of the hall – a truly dramatic, *just* not melodramatic, invention. There is the way the Corinthian order penetrates the building and comes out to a different sort of portico on the park side. To say any more would be straining to get too much out of one small illustration. But one thing you may already have noticed. Vanbrugh and Hawksmoor could never have made what they did of Blenheim without knowing – through engravings – what Bernini and his predecessors had done, on just about double the scale, at St Peter's half a century before. Compare Blenheim with the little air-view of St Peter's (Plate 44); the Doric wings of Blenheim with Bernini's colonnades; the giant order at Blenheim with Michelangelo's giant pilasters at St. Peter's (Plate 45).

Well, there are three buildings which, I believe, demonstrate with peculiar brilliance the 'rhetoric' of the Baroque. Yes, I think, 'rhetoric' is the key word. These buildings use the classical language of architecture with force and drama in order to overcome our resistance and persuade us into the truth of what they have to tell us – whether it is about the invincible glory of British arms, the paramount magnificence of Louis XIV, or the universal embrace of the Roman Church.

5. The Light of Reason – and of Archaeology

The use of the classical language of architecture has implied, at all times when it has risen to high eloquence, a certain philosophy. You cannot use the orders lovingly unless you love them; and you cannot love them without persuading yourself that they embody some absolute principle of truth or beauty. Belief in the fundamental authority of the orders has taken various forms, the simplest being in these terms: Rome was the greatest; Rome knew best. The sheer veneration of Rome is the clue to much in our civilization. It is a veneration we cannot easily share ourselves because we know too much about Rome and do not always like what we know; and also because we know far more than has ever been known before of other civilizations which ministered to the successes which Rome achieved. But to understand the mind of the fifteenth and sixteenth centuries we must, in this respect, be simple. There is a beautiful story told by Burckhardt of an occasion in 1485, when it was announced that the corpse of a Roman lady, in perfect preservation, had been discovered in an ancient sarcophagus. The corpse was taken to the Palazzo dei Conservatori and as the news spread people thronged to see this marvel. The Roman lady, her mouth and eyes half open, the colour still in her cheeks, was 'more beautiful', says a contemporary, 'than can be said or written and were it said or written, it would not be believed by those who had not seen her'. Of course, the thing was a fake. But the emotion was not. If the lady was Roman, people knew she must be beautiful beyond anything that any living person had ever seen.

That touching and unreasoning faith in Roman excellence belongs mostly to the fifteenth century. It comes over to us vividly in the little story I have just told you. It comes back with incredible force in some of the paintings of Mantegna in which senators, consuls, lictors and centurions, stand ready to re-enact their parts within an ambience of superb and glittering monuments.

But the simplicity of that faith made it vulnerable. If it inspired action, it also challenged enquiry and criticism; and criticism, while knowing and accepting the fact that Rome was best and greatest, demanded to know why? Why was Rome the fount of all goodness in architecture? One answer was, because all educated people everywhere agreed on the incomparable beauty of Roman architecture; but that merely begged the question. Another answer was that it enshrined certain mathematical rules to which all beauty was accountable; but that was not easy to prove. A third answer – and a much more profound one – was that Roman architecture had descended, through the Greeks, from the most primitive epoch of human history and was thus possessed of a sort of natural rightness – was indeed, almost a work of nature. Vitruvius was invoked to support this view. He taught that the Doric order developed from a timber prototype and from this it was argued that the original temples had had tree-trunks for columns and were thus derived from the primitive forests. A curious allusion to this belief occurs in some of the columns in the cloister of S. Ambrogio, Milan, designed by Bramante, where the shafts of the stone columns have the stumps of sawn-off branches carved on them.

But this question of 'why?' did not really worry anybody very much till the seventeenth century and then it was not in Italy but in France that the questioners appeared. It was natural, I suppose, that a critical spirit should emerge not in the homeland of classical architecture, Italy, but in a country where it had been absorbed and adapted and where it displaced the most intellectual of all medieval building traditions. Anyway, it was in France, about the middle of the seventeenth century, that questions began to be asked about the true nature of the orders and the way they should be used in modern buildings. The 'natural rightness' of the orders was accepted and the first concern of French critics was to ensure their purity and integrity. The new call to order came in a series of books. First, there was the famous *Parallèle*, the *Parallel of the Ancient Architecture with the Modern*, by Roland Fréart, which contains a minute comparison of the orders as found in antiquity and as interpreted by the theorists from Serlio onwards. Fréart pleads for rigorous selective purity. Then came the leading architect of the Louvre, Claude Perrault, with his beautiful and searchingly annotated edition of Vitruvius; likewise his treatise on the orders – the treatise from which I have borrowed Plate 2 as being perhaps the most elegant of all engraved presentations of the orders. And then, in 1706, followed a more remarkable book than any of these – a book by a French abbé, the abbé Cordemoy. On the face of it, Cordemoy's *Nouveau Traité*, his *New Treatise on the whole of Architecture*, seems to be just another critical review of the orders, tending in the same direction as his pre-decessors. But it is far more than that. Cordemoy wants not only to liberate the orders from every kind of distortion and affectation; he wants to get rid of the whole business of using the orders ornamentally – to get rid of what he calls, rather effectively, 'architecture in relief' – pilasters, half, three-quarter columns, attached columns, ornamental pediments, pedestals, attic storeys – the lot. His approach is a sort of primitive methodism, stripping away all the elaborate linguistics of architecture, all the mystery and drama, all the brilliant play of the Italian masters, and making the orders speak their own original functional language – no more, no less.

This approach was all very fine and much in line with French thought of the period; it was all very *rational* (which, of course, was the point) but it did not really work even in theory because the orders themselves, as found in Rome, are by no means primitive, by no means functional but, on the contrary, highly stylized. And it was left for another French abbé, the jesuit Laugier, nearly fifty years later, to announce a theory which really did upset the architectural apple-cart and shift the basis of architectural thought for a century to come. Perhaps more than a century; because I am not sure that Laugier may not justly be called the first modern architectural philosopher.

Now, the established hypothesis of all architectural theorists was that architecture had originated when primitive man built himself a primitive hut. From the hut he went on to the temple and, refining continually on the temple formula, he invented the timber version of the Doric and then copied it in stone. The other orders followed. That was the theory and everybody accepted it. But what nobody had done was to think at all concretely about the primitive hut; and this is what Laugier did. He visualised it. He visualised it as a structure consisting of upright posts, cross beams and a pitched roof – much what you see in the allegorical frontispiece to his book, reproduced in Plate 52. This, he declared, was the ultimate image of architectural truth, 'the model' (to use his own words) 'upon which all the magnificences of architecture have been imagined'.

Here, for the first time, the basis of authority of the orders was undermined – displaced by something else, by an image of their own hypothetical prototype, which is a functional, a rational prototype. Not that Laugier wanted to banish the orders; on the contrary, he believed that further orders might well be invented. But he wanted architects to use them with the same sense of constructional truth as the posts and beams in the primitive hut. He agreed with Cordemoy that all 'architecture in relief' must go, but he went further in wanting even walls to go. For Laugier, the ideal building consisted entirely of columns – columns carrying beams, carrying a roof.

This may, on the face of it, seem mildly funny – though to us in the mid-twentieth century, surrounded by brand-new buildings consisting of reinforced concrete columns with nothing but glass diaphragms between them, it should not seem funny so much as grandly prophetic. Anyway, in 1753, no *architect* could have proposed anything so crazy as the abolition of walls. But Laugier was not an architect; he was a philosopher and he was dealing in abstractions. He knew, of course, that walls could not be and would not be abolished, but he was establishing a principle of architectural beauty and that principle, he believed, had been revealed to him as quite necessarily an affair of columns. And it is not at all difficult to be with him in this. Look. A single column is just – well, a point on a plan; or rather, a very small circle on a plan – it gives you the module of an order but nothing more. But two columns give you at once an intercolumniation, therefore a rhythm and there, with the module, you have the germ of a whole building. The principle is as logically valid today as it was two hundred and ten years ago.

But what effect did Laugier's book, his *Essai sur l'Architecture*, have in 1753? In France it was devoured; in England and in Germany translations appeared within two years. It was discussed and attacked, digested or rejected all over Europe. In actual building I think it is fair to say that any fresh, innovating work after about 1755 is certain either to be coloured by Laugier's views or to show a positive rejection of them. The building which embodies his principles in the most spectacular degree is the Panthéon in Paris, of which there are illustrations in Plates 53 and 54. The Panthéon is now no longer a church but it was begun as one, dedicated to Ste Geneviève and the architect was Jacques-Germain Soufflot. Soufflot was not exactly a disciple of Laugier's but his own ideas on architectural principles ran close to Laugier's and were probably inflected by them. If you look at the exterior of the Panthéon, Plate 53, you may, I am afraid, be rather baffled by the fact that, contrary to everything Laugier advocated, it consists almost entirely of wall. But if you look carefully you will see grey oblong patches in the walls; and these are filled-in windows; Soufflot's intention, in fact, was more window than wall but his factor of safety proved too low: the windows had to be blocked. The interior is more to the point though, here again, unintended masonry had to be introduced to assure stability. Still, Soufflot's intention is perfectly clear and you feel it today the moment you enter that brittle and coldly exquisite building. He was trying to build a church in which the order, expressed only in the round, only in independent, cylindrical shafts, not only looked very beautiful but actually did the whole work of carrying the roof. He very nearly succeeded.

Now this is a very long way from another church I described in these talks – Palladio's Redentore in Venice (Plate 17). You may remember that when I described the Redentore I made a special point of the *articulation* of the orders. If Palladio made a virtue of articulation, Soufflot made it quintessential. To put these two churches side by side is to see exactly the difference in ideals between the mid-sixteenth century and the mid-eighteenth. Palladio was trying, above all things, to be truly Roman. Soufflot was trying to be something altogether more philosophical – trying to reach the truth behind Rome, the combined structural and aesthetic truth which the orders, in their origin, could be supposed to have embodied.

The Panthéon is the first major building which can be called neo-classical – 'neo-classical' being the expression which has come to be used for architecture which, on the one hand, tends towards the rational simplification advocated by Cordemoy and Laugier and, on the other hand, seeks to present the orders with the utmost antiquarian fidelity. Reason and archaeology are the two complementary elements which make Neo-classicism and which differentiate it from the Baroque. Or do they? Once again I must warn you against giving too exact a meaning to these labels. Just think back to one of the major Baroque works I described in the previous chapter – Bernini's Piazza in front of St Peter's (Plate 46). What, you may say, could possibly be truer to Laugier's ideal than those giant crescents consisting wholly of independent columns, innocent of all modelling and enrichment. Yes, indeed. As so often happens, the expression of a new ideal had involuntarily presented itself, on one particular occasion, fully fledged, long before it occurred to anybody to formulate the new ideal in words.

Something of this sort happened also in English architecture even earlier and in a peculiarly striking way. Look at Plate 19 – Inigo Jones's church of St Paul, Covent Garden. It was built in 1631, but if it is not pure neo-classicism I do not know what is. It is a study in the primitive, based on Vitruvius's description of the Tuscan. That fine, spreading roof, those massive wide-spaced columns are almost pure archaeology, *and* about as basically structural as you can get – in fact, well on the way to the primitive hut. A hundred years later, but still well before Laugier's formulation of the new theory, the English were acknowledging Jones's leadership in this direction, one perhaps somewhat over-enthusiastic critic of 1734 describing the Covent Garden church as 'without a rival, one of the most perfect pieces of architecture that the art of man can produce'. If one is in sympathy with the Neo-classical ideal one can see what he meant. And this was written only a year or two after Lord Burlington had paid *his* respects to Vitruvian archaeology by building the Assembly Room at York (Plate 20), a perfect reconstruction of the 'Oecus Aegyptius' or Egyptian Hall – a Vitruvian model illustrated from Palladio's wood-cut (Plate 18).

I do not suppose that Laugier had heard of either of these buildings, but Soufflot obviously – and I think you will already have noticed this – knew something of English architecture because he took St Paul's dome as his model for the dome of the Panthéon. You can judge for yourself whether you think the imitation an entire success. To my mind, the narrower intercolumniation of the Panthéon and the elimination of the solid piers in every fourth bay, results in a loss of gravity: the Panthéon dome spins rather too airily over the rectangles of the cross-shaped structure below. Soufflot, no doubt, thought he was purifying Wren's design – getting rid of what Cordemoy would have called 'architecture in relief' and seizing only the essentials.

The actual impact of Laugier on English architecture is another story and an important one. The English already had – as we have just seen – a strong tradition of architectural puritanism, appearing first in Inigo Jones, cropping up again and again, even sometimes in Wren and Hawksmoor, and implicit in the English eighteenth century addiction to Palladio. But perhaps the very fact that the English had this rather puritanical attitude to architecture made them reluctant to go all the way with Laugier. Besides, the English were, under the skin, incurably romantic; and if the rationalism of Laugier pulled in one direction, the wildly irrational inventions of the great architect-etcher, Giambattista Piranesi, pulled in another. The imagination of Piranesi was irresistible. Look at Plate 49, one of Piranesi's famous prison scenes – a cavernous perspective of Roman arches, chipped and scarred, dripping with horror, and rusticated more wildly than anything at Mantua. An architect could hardly, you would think, have *both* Laugier and Piranesi for his heroes.

And yet that is very much what some English architects did – George Dance for instance, whose Newgate Prison (Plate 49) is obviously in the mood of Piranesi but some of whose other works are just as clearly influenced by Laugier. The establishment, on the whole, was against Laugier. Sir William Chambers, the author of the one great English eighteenth-century treatise on architecture, objected both to the thesis of the primitive hut and to the sweeping elimination of everything except columns in the round. And yet in the plate in Chambers's book where he illustrates the development of the Doric order, reproduced in Plate 55, are two versions of the primitive hut which must surely have been sketched after a reading of Laugier.

Whatever the actual effect of Laugier's thought in England, the idea of primitivism, of searching back to the true, untainted sources of architectural beauty, certainly prevailed in this country and it had two main results. One of these was the Greek Revival. The other was the peculiar, idiosyncratic primitivism of Sir John Soane.

The Greek Revival is something in which England played a very special part. Till the middle of the eighteenth century Greek architecture was something of a mystery. Everybody knew that the Romans had got their architecture from the Greeks and if it was a question of looking for 'untainted sources' Greece was obviously the place to look. But nobody ever went to Greece. It was a long way off; it was part of the Ottoman Empire and neither an easy nor a safe place for the western traveller. However, in 1751 two Englishmen, James Stuart and Nicholas Revett, set out for Athens; they came back three years later and in 1762 the first volume of their book, containing accurate measured drawings of Greek buildings, was published. A Frenchman, Le Roy, forestalled them with a more pictorial book in 1758, but Stuart and

Revett became the acknowledged authorities.

When people saw, for the first time, accurate representations of the Parthenon and the Theseion – the major examples of the Greek Doric order of the age of Pericles – what did they think of them? Were they coarser and cruder than Roman Doric, because earlier in date; or were they purer because nearer the source? It all depended on what one was looking for. Some saw them as one thing, some as another. You see, Greek Doric (of which Plate 57 gives a fair imitated example) *is* squatter and more massive than the Roman (compare the Roman Doric column in Plate 55). On the other hand its profiles are more tense and subtle. Some latitude of interpretation was inevitable. The first Greek Doric buildings built in England were built more or less as curiosities, exotic souvenirs, in the form of temples and porches on gentlemen's estates. But about the turn of the century the conviction that the Greek Doric – and Greek Ionic and Greek Corinthian – were in all ways purer and better than their Roman counterparts had won the day and the Greek Revival proper had started. There were now not five orders to choose from but eight – the five Roman orders established long ago by Serlio, and the three Greek orders which could be extracted from Stuart and Revett. The Revivalists, of course, confined themselves to these.

The Greek Revival, which started in England, eventually manifested itself all over Europe and quickly spread to America. It lasted for about thirty years and I do not think anybody would consider it one of the more glorious episodes in architectural history. The Greek orders always remained curiosities – specimens brought out of a museum. Since the Greeks had never evolved the daring mechanics of style which the Romans had done, since the Greeks never used the arch or the vault or built huge multistorey buildings, the revived Greek elements tended to be used as cumbersome and costly appendages to modern buildings of otherwise rather negative character. Look again at the photograph of the High School at Edinburgh (Plate 57), built in 1825 – certainly a most spectacular and persuasive Greek Doric performance, beautifully sited on Calton Hill. But I really believe that if all this architecture were taken away the High School as a functioning building would still be there – and it would get a great deal more light. Much the same could be said of the British Museum, illustrated on page 47, bottom right. Of course, I know this is not quite fair. 'Useless' porticos and 'useless' colonnades are perfectly legitimate means of architectural expression, but when they become a sort of cultural luggage carried by buildings which they screen, cover and adorn but do not really control a very dead dead-end has been reached.

Now Sir John Soane, who had one of the most original and explorative minds of the period which saw the Greek Revival, never committed himself to anything of this kind. He always designed his buildings from inside out. He knew his Greek orders very well. He knew his Roman orders even better. He knew his Italians. He had a keen appreciation of Laugier. And knowing all this he was able to go to the root of the matter and make his own statements as to the fundamentals of architecture. Laugier's primitivism – the idea of going back to pre-historic beginnings – certainly appealed to him but he was prepared to go much further than Laugier in actually eliminating all the conventional orders from his practice and inventing a 'primitive' order of his own. You can see it at his Dulwich Art Gallery, which still stands, and of which a drawing, from the Soane Museum, is illustrated in Plate 56. Soane's 'order' here is nothing but a brick pier or a brick strip with a stone necking and a stone projection over it which is a token cornice. He did not share Laugier's hostility to pilasters. Soane's critics made fun of this order by calling it his 'Bœotian' order. There is not a single conventional column or even a conventional moulding in sight. Everything has been abstracted and then rendered back in Soane's own personal interpretation. It is all very original and seems to point to a new freedom for architecture. It seems so to us, but it did not to the generation that followed.

When he died, his style died with him and nobody was sorry. The Greek Revival was dying too. Laugier and his ideas were forgotten. It might seem that the story of the classical language of architecture was finished.

But it was not. Whether the story of that language ever was or ever will be finished I do not know. But in my next talk, which will also be my last, I shall go deeper into what I called in my first talk the essentials of classicism. Because these penetrated the stylistic chaos of the nineteenth century and became the vital factors in the architectural revolution of the twentieth – the revolution which gave us the architecture which we use today.

6. Classical into Modern

In the last fifty years the architectural habits of the world have changed completely. Within that period and at the heart of the process of change we can now trace as a matter of history, the workings of what it is still natural to call the Modern Movement in architecture. The Modern Movement had its beginnings in the decade before 1914. It reached its highest pitch of creative vigour in the late 'twenties. After World War II, it ceased to move; not because the war killed it but because the war had rendered its universal acceptance inevitable. Its *effects* spread and spread with undiminishing momentum until by now there is no corner of the indus-

trialized world in which the thin, high glossy blocks, the perspectives of concrete posts, the eternally repeating rectangles are not typical and familiar. Today one would hardly cross the road to look at a building whose kind thirty years ago, drew one across Europe with excited anticipation to see, photograph and write home about.

Such is the architectural revolution of our century. And it is, I think, complete. Fashions eddy across the surface of things, brilliant individual performances make spectacular rings, but the revolution is done with, spent. Questions of form in architecture are tending to recede, giving place to questions of technology and industrialization, planning and mass-production for social needs – questions of building rather than architecture; and it is even a matter for debate whether architecture will retain its traditional status much longer, or dissolve into a close federation of town-planning, structural engineering and industrial design.

There is nothing to deplore about all this – in fact, there is much to hope for in this transformation which is, in effect, the full arrival of a new man-made environment – one which has been predicted for a long time. The only reason I make any mention of these things here is in order to ask, against this sweeping background, the rather simple-minded question, 'Where now is the classical language of architecture?'

Well, obviously, it is not here, is it? Has it then any relevance? Let us ask another question – 'What *is* modern architecture?' You can answer that question, if you like, with a few platitudes about form and function. But they will not really do; and if you are going to describe what modern architecture is, you can only do so by describing the achievements of specific innovating personalities, their time and space relationships and their progressive disturbance of the general drift of architectural theory and practice. The roots of modern architecture are in the thought and in the performance of these leaders and the thought and performance of these leaders is inextricably involved with their reactions to, their alliance with and departures from the classical traditions of their own and earlier centuries. Not only that, but within these consecutive traditions there are persistent foreshadowings of the modern, from the middle of the eighteenth century onwards. In short, an exact understanding of what we so vaguely and airily call modern can only come

through an understanding of its classical parentage and it is this function of the classical language that I want to put before you now.

You will remember that in my last talk I said something of the architectural philosophy of the Abbé Laugier – the man who set before the world the image of the primitive hut or 'rustic cabin' as the ultimate source of all architectural beauty. This image was rather quaint – it consisted simply of four tree trunks with branches set across them for beams and more branches for rafters; and it had no walls. As a building of this kind would be quite useless to anybody, however primitive, it may be assumed that it never existed except in Laugier's imagination. It had no more archaeological sanction than Rousseau's Noble Savage (who came on the literary scene a few years later) had anthropological sanction. It was, in fact, a symbolic diagram; and the meaning of it was that behind Rome, behind Greece there was a *principle* which was, as it were, pure essence of architecture.

There were implications here which I do not think Laugier himself realized and which took a very long time indeed to unfold. If the primitive hut was 'pure' architecture, did that mean that it was a one hundred per cent efficient solution of a specific problem of shelter? Obviously not. Or did it mean that 'pure' architecture was limited to columns, beams and rafters? That does seem to have been in Laugier's mind and to that extent his primitive hut was simply a reduction to the lowest possible terms of the classical temple form – an expression still well within the classical language of architecture. On the other hand it contained the germ of the *rational* – the column merely a cylindrical post – the pediment merely a built-up triangle; it contained, in fact, the germ of an architecture from which all decorative and plastic expressions were removed and which (once the tree-trunks were given a bit of polish) was strictly an affair of solid geometry. But it was still architecture.

Such an architecture did come into being – or very nearly – towards the end of the eighteenth century. It mostly had rather Utopian implications and one of its most astonishing manifestations is in the ideal city conceived, designed, never executed, but published, in 1805, by the French architect Ledoux. This is a dream city for a dream society and contains some projects as surprising in their purpose as their form. Plate 58 is one of them. It is a centre for the sexual instruction of adolescents – a very high-minded affair, let me say – with an elaborate programme which need not concern us here. But look at the geometry of it – a complex but harmonious disposition of solids in beautiful relation to the landscape. Irresistibly one is reminded of the definition of architecture which Le Corbusier wrote in 1921 – 'the play of volumes, disposed with masterly and superb exactitude beneath the light'. Le Corbusier also projected an ideal city – his Ville Radieuse – and it is not surprising that in the nineteen-twenties an architectural scholar thought it worth writing a book drawing an analogy between the two utopias – Ledoux's and Le Corbusier's. This is not to say that Le Corbusier was influenced by Ledoux. So far as I know he was not.

Ledoux's passion for seeing buildings as aggregates of simple geometrical shapes was shared by some others of his time and a little later – the German, Karl Friedrich Schinkel, for instance, whose old Museum at Berlin is illustrated in Plate 59. Here the shapes are very simple but enormously effective.

They consist mainly of a rectangular mass, one of whose sides is a transparent screen of columns. These are seen against an inner wall, but behind this wall rises, in the middle, the cubic form of the central hall of the Museum. A simple but very powerful three-dimensional combination indeed, beside which the British Museum (Plate 60), for all the splendour of its colonnades, cuts a rather poor figure. For the British Museum is all colonnade – there is not a single architectural clue to the building behind it, which, so far as the onlooker from outside is concerned, might almost as well not be there.

Now, although I have underlined the importance of pure solid geometry in the Ledoux design and in Schinkel's museum, it will not have escaped you that in both of them architectural orders are present – in the Ledoux design as a Greek portico at one end of the building controlling its main lines and echoed at the other end by a semi-circular colonnade; in the museum, as a spectacular and beautifully detailed colonnade which has great formal importance in the whole design. The language of classical architecture is still very much alive and the orders are still not only present but in control. Although we may seem, here, to be on the threshold of modern architecture, that threshold was to take a long time to cross. Most of the nineteenth and part of the twentieth centuries stood between.

The nineteenth century was very much concerned – over-concerned we may think – with the historical styles. Classical buildings were continually being built but they always looked back, not merely to Greece and Rome but to nearly every succeeding phase of classical development, using the past as one glorious quarry of ideas. C. R. Cockerell, in his New

Ashmolean building at Oxford, which we looked at earlier on (Plate 35), wove into his design ornaments from Greek temples, a columnar arrangement from the Roman triumphal arch, a cornice from Vignola and other elements from sources as far apart as Florentine mannerism and Nicholas Hawksmoor. Similarly, Charles Garnier's Paris Opera House (Plate 61), built twenty years later than the Ashmolean, contains a basic idea by Bramante, the Louvre colonnade – into which is intruded a subsidiary order on Michelangelo's Capitoline principle – some parts of the earlier Louvre and a Roman attic storey. Classical designers were, so to speak, circling round the achievements of the past looking for things which could be done again in a different way or in different combinations.

Meanwhile, the lively and progressive thought of the age of Laugier took what we may think a rather odd turning. To Frenchmen, however classically minded, it was never quite possible to ignore the fact that some of the most daring, powerful and ingenious buildings ever built were the medieval cathedrals standing on their own soil. The French never had quite the nostalgic, parochial reverence for Gothic which the English had; they admired it as engineering. And admiring it thus – for the structural economy and completeness represented by a vaulted church – it was perhaps inevitable that the idea of a rational architecture should be transferred from an interest in classical antiquity to an interest in the middle ages. Anyway, the greatest French theorist of the nineteenth century – Eugène Viollet-le-Duc – spent most of his life elucidating Gothic architecture as a completely rational way of building and then issuing, in his lectures, a challenge to the modern world to create a modern architecture out of iron and glass, as well as timber and masonry – an architecture just as economical, as rational, as the Gothic. His challenge was met in various ways. The experimental Art Nouveau of the 'nineties contains several attempted answers to the problems he posed. But none of them really worked – they were far-fetched and smelt too much of the studio. The real answers were to come after all, not from an ingenious and really rather precarious philosophy of Gothic, but from the classical tradition which all Europe had shared with antiquity for so long.

The story of what I suppose will always be called the 'Modern Movement' in architecture has been written several times and is likely to be re-written many times more. Here, my only business with that complex and involved piece of history is to show how and to what extent the classical language which has been the subject of these talks entered into it, what effect it had and how much of that effect remains. The most direct way of doing this will be to go straight to the work of two great pioneers of the first generation of moderns – the German, Peter Behrens, who was born in 1868; and the Frenchman, Auguste Perret, born in 1873. Buildings by both are illustrated (Plates 62 and 63).

Peter Behrens, who started as a painter, was one of the leaders of the German arts and crafts movement of the early nineteen-hundreds. The great electrical combine, A.E.G., appointed him their architect and artistic adviser and in 1908 commissioned him to design a turbine erection hall for their factory in Berlin (Plate 62). Behrens was faced here with the problem of designing a building for a strictly industrial purpose, but at the same time giving it the 'prestige' character which the company expected of their architect. It was typical

43

of German thought at this time that Behrens should look back to German neo-classicism and the age of Karl-Friedrich Schinkel, whose Berlin museum we were considering just now. The turbine hall is really a neo-classical building designed on the lines of a temple but with all the stylistic signs and symbols left out or changed. You may remember, from my last talk, that Sir John Soane was doing something like this more than a hundred years earlier. And in a sense Behrens in 1908 was not much more advanced than Soane (at Dulwich) in 1811. Except for this: Soane was working out his style in traditional and (so far as he could see) unchanging materials; while Behrens had to accept the challenge of structural steel, a material which, if its economic dictatorship was not accepted, would soon put architects out of business. So in the turbine hall the classical colonnade is represented by those unmodulated verticals on the flank of the building which are in fact steel stanchions. The temple portico has shrunk into one great window area, under a 'pediment' which is not triangular but multangular to suit the structure of the roof behind it. At the corners are plain wall surfaces with horizontal lines on them which seem to be a vestigial kind of rustication. None of this would 'tell' in quite the splendid way it does if Behrens had not adopted the device of 'battering' – that is to say leaning in – his solid wall in the same leaning plane as the windows along the side. To what extent this device is purely aesthetic I do not know but it gives relief and shadow at the eaves of the roof in just the place where in a temple we should have the relief and shadow of the cornice.

Behrens' turbine hall is a great performance but not a kind of performance that could be repeated very often. The chal-lenge of steel had to be more directly and economically met and it was Walter Gropius, a pupil of Behrens, who took the next step, moving a good deal further from the neo-classical model but without losing aesthetic integrity or, indeed, the sense of classical order and symmetry. The pre-first-war industrial buildings of Gropius as well as those of Behrens are key monuments of the Modern Movement.

Now turn from Behrens and his pupil Gropius to the Frenchman – Auguste Perret. Here was an entirely different kind of designer. Perret had no need, or desire, to look back to the neo-classicism of the early nineteenth century; as a Frenchman he had in his bones, so to speak, the still living tradition of classical design fostered by the École des Beaux Arts, that school of design whose most obviously representative building is, I suppose, the Paris Opera-house. I think if you glance again at the Opera (Plate 61) and then at the building by Perret on the same page (bottom right) you will see a certain connection. Perret's Naval Construction Depot is all in reinforced concrete, totally without enrichment. But it is thought out in terms of 'orders' – a major order starting from the ground and running up to something rather like an architrave and cornice; and the ghost of a secondary order whose entablature belongs just above the heads of the first-floor windows. There is almost as much 'relief' and almost as much variety of rhythm in this building as in the Opera-house. Only there are no mouldings and there is no carving.

In those buildings by two masters of the Modern Movement we have two statements regarding the possible interpretation of the classical language in terms of steel (Behrens) and reinforced concrete (Perret). Buildings such as these claimed in their day a new freedom, unrelated to specific orders and yet still closely related to the rhythms and general disposition of classical architecture. There was no reason at all why this kind of diagrammatic classicism should not prevail indefinitely as the medium for new constructions – indeed, plenty of buildings are still being built very close in expression to Perret's work of the 'twenties. But it happened otherwise, chiefly through the creative genius of one man – Le Corbusier – the most inventive mind in the architecture of our time and also, in a curious way, one of the most classical minds.

Le Corbusier was born in 1887. In 1908-9 he was for a short time in Perret's office in Paris; in 1910 to 1911 he spent a few months in Germany with Behrens. His first house, built in Switzerland during World War I, showed the influence of these masters, especially of Perret. After the war he turned to painting and was involved, along with Amédée Ozenfant, in a movement they called Purism whose aim was to bring a mathematical discipline to bear on what they saw as the imminent disintegration of cubism. In 1920 Le Corbusier started writing – about architecture. His collected articles were made up into a book, published in 1923, the famous *Vers une Architecture* – 'Towards an architecture' – probably the most widely circulated and influential architectural book of our time.

Now, one way of putting Le Corbusier's architectural achievement in a nutshell would be to say that he completely reversed modern architecture as he found it – he turned it upside down. He found men like Behrens and Perret subduing the chaos of empirical engineering and industrial building by disciplining it into a classically designed framework. Le Corbusier threw away this framework and let the industrial forms speak their own, often bizarre, language; but he exercised a more formidable and effective control than the token orders of Behrens and Perret could do by the application of what he has called 'tracés regulateurs' – lines of control. In doing this, Le Corbusier was re-assuming a kind of control which had never been entirely forgotten but which belongs essentially to the Renaissance and was fundamental to the work both of Alberti and of Palladio.

At the base of this kind of control is the conviction that harmonious relationships in architecture can only be secured if the shapes of rooms and the openings in walls and indeed all elements in a building are made to conform with certain ratios which are related continuously to all other ratios in the building. To what extent rational systems of this kind do produce effects which eye and mind can consciously apprehend I am extremely doubtful. I have a feeling that the real point of such systems is simply that their users (who are mostly their authors) need them; that there are types of extremely fertile, inventive mind which need the tough inexorable discipline of such systems to correct and at the same time stimulate invention. And the fate of these systems seems, on the whole, to confirm this; they rarely survive their authors and users and the next man of fertile genius invents his own. That, however, in no way diminishes their importance.

In the first talk in this series I said that 'the aim of classical architecture has always been to achieve a demonstrable harmony of parts'. Perhaps the word 'demonstrable' should not have been quite so closely linked with 'always'. Nevertheless a demonstrable harmony – one which results from a specific code to which reference can be made – is something which conforms absolutely with the nature of classicism and lies very close to the use of the orders which are in themselves demonstrations of harmonious composition. For Le Corbusier the demonstration of the harmonious was always extremely important. Even his first Perret-style house of 1916 he published with the 'tracés regulateurs' ruled across the elevations. The Purist manifesto ran in the same direction and the 'tracés' are dealt with – if rather superficially – in a chapter of *Vers une Architecture*. But it was not till the early years of World War II that Le Corbusier created the system which he used in all his later work – the system which he has called the 'Modulor'. 'Modulor' is a word made out of 'module' (that is to say, unit of measurement) and 'section d'or' or golden section – otherwise mean and extreme ratio: that is to say the division of a line so that the larger part is to the whole line as the smaller part to the larger. The Modulor is a system of space-notation based on this geometrical absolute and constituting a 'gamut' of dimensions. A middle phase of the gamut relates to the dimensions of the human body; the other phases extend it to the minutiae of precision instruments on the one hand and to the scale of vast town-planning enterprises on the other.

Le Corbusier made enormous claims for the Modulor as a system which, if widely adopted, could solve many of the standardization problems of industry and promote harmony throughout our whole physical environment into the bargain. Perhaps it could; but the fact is that, since its publication in 1950, interest in it has rather receded and I am inclined to think that, in this case as in so many others, the real importance of the thing was as part of its author's mental furniture – enabling him to embark on projects as wildly original, for instance, as his chapel at Ronchamp – a building so free in form as to be practically abstract sculpture – always secure in his complete grasp of rational procedure.

'Rational procedure'. That is perhaps the last, and certainly not the least legacy of classicism to the architecture of our own time: rational procedure controlling – and inciting – invention. That has always been and is always likely to be the way architectural creation works. And of this process the history of the classical language of architecture provides the immemorial, the most universal and explicit model.

Glossary

ABACUS The top part of any capital; as it were a square slab placed on top of the capital to bear the beam (architrave).

ABUTMENT The solid mass from which an arch springs.

ACANTHUS The plant of which a highly conventionalized version decorates the capitals of the Corinthian and Composite orders.

ACROTERIA Small pedestals (originally for sculpture but often seen without) at the extremities and apex of a pediment.

AEDICULE The architectural frame of an opening, consisting usually of two columns supporting an entablature and pediment.

AMPHIPROSTYLE See TEMPLE.

ANTA Equivalent to PILASTER where the latter is the respond to a column. Mostly applied to Greek architecture, where the anta capital is different from that of the columns accompanying it.

ARAEOSTYLE See INTERCOLUMNIATION.

ARCHITRAVE The lowest of the three primary divisions of the ENTABLATURE. The word is loosely applied to any moulding round a door or window and such mouldings do, in fact, most frequently borrow the profile of the architrave in the strict sense.

ARCHITRAVE-CORNICE An entablature from which the frieze is elided.

ARCHIVOLT An architrave moulding when it follows the line of an arch.

ASTRAGAL A small moulding of circular profile.

ATTIC BASE See BASE.

ATTIC STOREY A storey placed over the main entablature of a building and in strictly architectural relation to it (as e.g. in some triumphal arches).

BASE (of a column) There are three main varieties. (i) The Attic Base, the commonest, which is found with all orders except the Tuscan; it consists of two tori separated by a scotia and fillets. (ii) The Tuscan Base, consisting simply of a torus and fillet. (iii) A type consisting of two scotiae separated by two astragals with a torus above and a torus below. This, with variations of it, is applicable to the Ionic, Corinthian and Composite.

BEAD-AND-REEL See ENRICHMENTS.

BED MOULDINGS The mouldings between the corona (q.v.) and the frieze (q.v.) in any entablature.

BUKRANIA Carved representations of ox skulls, often found in the metopes of the Doric frieze.

CAPITAL (of a column) Each of the five orders has its appropriate capital. Those of the Tuscan and (Roman) Doric are much alike, consisting mainly of abacus, ovolo and, further down, an astragal; the Doric has more multiplicity of small mouldings than the Tuscan. The Ionic is distinguished by *volutes*. These are the coiled ends of an element inserted between the abacus and the ovolo. Sometimes, however, the volutes spring separately from the ovolo. The Corinthian capital is decorated with two ranks of acanthus leaves, while fern-like stems reach out to the corners of the abacus. The Composite capital combines Corinthian leaves with Ionic volutes.

CARYATIDES Female figures supporting an entablature. The most famous example is at the Erectheum, Athens, where Vitruvius improbably supposed the figures to represent Carian captives, hence the generic name.

CAVETTO A hollow moulding, whose profile is usually a quarter of a circle.

COLOSSAL ORDER Any order whose columns extend from the ground through several storeys.

COMPOSITE ORDER This order, which combines features of the Ionic with the Corinthian, is not described by Vitruvius and was probably evolved after his time. It was first identified by Alberti (c. 1450) and first figured by Serlio as the fifth and most elaborate of the five orders.

CONSOLE A bracket in the form of an S-shaped scroll, with one end broader than the other. A console has many applications, either vertical (e.g. against a wall to carry a bust) or horizontal (as the visible part of a cantilever supporting a gallery). Key-stones of arches are often modelled as consoles.

CORINTHIAN ORDER This order was an Athenian invention of the fifth century B.C. but in early examples is only differentiated from the Ionic by its leaf-enfurled capital. Even Vitruvius, in the first century A.D., described only the capital 'because the Corinthian order has not separate rules for the cornices and other ornaments'. However, in later Roman practice the Corinthian entablature crystallized as something quite distinct. The original design of the capital is attributed by Vitruvius to the sculptor Calli-machus who, he says, was inspired by the sight of a basket of toys placed, with a stone slab for protection (the abacus), on the grave of a Corinthian girl and around which wild acanthus had grown. The Corinthian order, as employed from the sixteenth century onwards, is based on Roman examples, notably the temples of Vespasian and Castor and Pollux in the Forum.

CORNICE The uppermost of the three primary divisions of the ENTABLATURE (q.v.) The word is loosely applied to almost any horizontal moulding forming a main decorative feature, especially to a moulding at the junction of walls and ceiling in a room. Such mouldings do, traditionally, follow the profiles of cornices in the strict sense.

CORONA The part of a cornice forming a sudden projection over the bed-moulding (q.v.).

CYMA RECTA A moulding which is concave in its upper part and convex below.

CYMA REVERSA A moulding which is convex in its upper part and concave below.

DECASTYLE See PORTICO.

DENTILS Small closely-spaced blocks forming one of the members of a cornice in the Ionic, Corinthian, Composite and, more rarely, Doric orders.

DIASTYLE See INTERCOLUMNIATION.

DIPTERAL See TEMPLE.

DISTYLE IN ANTIS A disposition comprising two columns between pilasters or antae.

DODECASTYLE See PORTICO.

DORIC ORDER The Greek Doric and Roman Doric both have, ultimately, a Greek origin but they developed in different ways. They have in common (i) the presence of triglyphs in the frieze, with mutules and guttae on the soffit of the corona and (ii) the fact that the capital consists of little more than an abacus supported by a moulding or mouldings. The Greek order has no base, nor is a base prescribed by Vitruvius, though in practice the Roman Doric always has a base, the Greek never. As full knowledge and appreciation of the Greek order was only regained in the late eighteenth century its appearance in the modern world before *c.* 1800 is rare.

ECHINUS See OVOLO.

EGG-AND-DART See ENRICHMENTS.

ENRICHMENTS Certain standard types of carved enrichment are appropriate to certain standard profiles. Thus, the ovolo is enriched with *egg-and-dart*, the cyma reversa with *water-leaf*, the bead or astragal with *bead-and-reel*. For the cyma recta, less frequently enriched, laurel leaves or honey-suckle are appropriate. In other elements of the order there is a wide margin of choice in enrichment.

ENTABLATURE The whole assemblage of parts supported by the column. The three primary divisions are ARCHITRAVE, FRIEZE and CORNICE. Of these, only the architrave and cornice are subdivided.

ENTASIS The swelling of a column. All classical columns are broader at the base than at the capital. The diminution often begins one third of the way up the column and thereafter takes the form of a curve whose setting-out is prescribed in various ways.

EUSTYLE See INTERCOLUMNIATION.

FASCIA A plain horizontal band. A common form of architrave consists of two or three fasciae each slightly oversailing the one below and perhaps separated from it by a narrow moulding.

FILLET A narrow horizontal strip separating the larger curved mouldings in a cornice or base.

FLUTING Vertical channels, of ounded section, cut in the shafts of columns. Never found in the Tuscan and optional in the other orders. Sometimes the lower flutings are filled with solid cylindrical pieces; they are then described as *cabled* flutings.

FRIEZE The middle of the three primary divisions of the ENTABLATURE. In essence the frieze is a plain horizontal band between the elaborately shelving cornice above and the architrave (which may or may not be divided into fasciae) below. But the Doric frieze usually contains triglyphs; while in the Ionic, Corinthian and Composite orders, the frieze is often appropriated to figure sculpture.

GUTTAE Small conical pieces carved on the architrave below the taenia under each triglyph in the Doric order. They evidently represent wooden pegs and thus originate, as does the triglyph, in the timber prototypes of the Doric.

HEXASTYLE See PORTICO.

IMPOST The moulding of a pier at the springing of an arch.

INTERCOLUMNIATION The distance, measured in diameters, between two columns. The types named by Vitruvius, with the ratios later assigned to them, are as follows: *Pycnostyle*, $1\frac{1}{2}$D; *Systyle*, 2 D; *Eustyle*, $2\frac{1}{4}$D; *Diasytle*, 3 D; *Araeostyle*, 4 D. Other intercolumniations are found in the Doric order where spacing is necessarily controlled by the triglyph-metope rhythm in the frieze. Eustyle intercolumniation is the most common.

IONIC ORDER This order, which originated in Asia Minor about the middle of the sixth century B.C. is distinguished in Roman examples by two main characteristics: (i) the voluted capital; (ii) the presence of dentils in the cornice. Vitruvius gives a minute description of the order.

METOPE The square space between two triglyphs in the frieze of the Doric order. Often left plain but sometimes decorated with bukrania, trophies or other ornaments.

MODILION An ornament in the cornice of the Corinthian and Composite orders. A modilion is a diminutive CONSOLE or scrolled bracket and the modilions in a cornice give the appearance of supporting the corona. They are spaced so as to allow a square sinking in the soffit between each pair.

MODULE The relative sizes of all parts of an order are traditionally given in Modules, a Module being half the diameter of the column just above its moulded base. The Module is divided into thirty minutes. Sometimes the diameter itself is called the Module, in which case it contains sixty minutes.

MUTULE A square block carved on the soffit of the Corona in the Doric order immediately over each triglyph. See TRIGLYPH.

OCTASTYLE See PORTICO.

ORDER An order is the total assemblage of parts comprising the column and its appropriate entablature. The primary divisions of the column are base, shaft and capital. The primary divisions of the entablature are architrave, frieze and cornice. A pedestal under the column is not an essential part of the order but appropriate pedestals are given by the theorists from Serlio onwards.

OVOLO A convex moulding whose profile is usually a quarter of a circle.

PALLADIAN MOTIF The name given by the French (*motif Palladio*) to the combination of arch and columns conspicuously illustrated in Palladio's Basilica at Vicenza (Fig. I). In principle the arrangement consists of an opening where an arch stands over columns whose entablatures are the lintels of narrower side openings (see VENETIAN WINDOW). In Palladio's Basilica this triple opening is framed in the bays formed by a superior order and it is to this system that the term 'Palladian Motif' should be confined.

Fig. I

PEDESTAL A substructure under a column. See ORDER.

PEDIMENT The triangular space created by the sloping eaves and horizontal cornice line of a gabled temple or other classical building. The word appears to be an alteration of *periment*, the word used in sixteenth century English accounts and perhaps deriving from French *parement*, facing. Pediments do not always express the end of a roof but are often used ornamentally, even on a large scale. On a miniature scale they commonly surmount door and window openings. There are many varieties and distortions of the pediment, e.g. the pediment with a curved (segmental) instead of pointed top, and the 'broken pediment' whose sloping sides are returned before reaching the apex.

PERIPTERAL See TEMPLE.

PERISTYLE A continuous colonnade surrounding a temple or court.

PIER The solids between door, window or other openings. Piers are invariably part of the carrying structure of a building. They may or may not be combined or overlaid with pilasters, half-columns, three-quarter columns, etc.

PILASTER The representation in relief of a column against a wall. The pilaster is sometimes considered as the visible part of a square column built into the wall. Pilasters are necessarily ornamental. They have a quasi-structural function, however, when acting as *responds*, i.e. as the thickening of a wall opposite a column whose entablature carries over to the wall.

PILLAR A word in common use which has no specific meaning in the context of classical architecture.

PLINTH The square solid under the base of a column or pedestal.

PODIUM A structure, usually massive, providing a platform on which a classical building is placed.

PORTICO A place for walking under shelter. The word is usually applied to the columned project on before the entrance to a temple or similar building. Porticos of this kind are described according to the number of frontal columns viz. *Tetrastyle* (4), *Hexastyle* (6), *Octastyle* (8), *Decastyle* (10) and *Dodecastyle* (12). Where there are only two columns between pilasters or antae the expression used in *Distyle in Antis*.

PROSTYLE See TEMPLE.

PSEUDODIPTERAL See TEMPLE.

PSEUDOPERIPTERAL See TEMPLE.

PYCNOSTYLE See INTERCOLUMNIATION.

QUOINS Usually the external angles of buildings, especially when these are emphasized by rustication.

RUSTICATION Masonry (or an imitation thereof) where the joints between the stones are deliberately emphasized by sinkings or where the stones are left rough or worked in such a way as to afford a striking textural effect.

SCOTIA A hollow moulding, most often seen between the tori in bases of columns.

SHAFT That part of a column which is between the base and the capital.

SOFFIT The under-side of any architectural element, e.g. a corona, or an architrave where it does not rest on columns.

STYLOBATE The steps under a portico or colonnade.

SYSTYLE See INTERCOLUMNIATION.

TAENIA The narrow projecting band between architrave and frieze in the Doric order.

TEMPLE The disposition of columns around temples has given rise to the following nomenclature. A temple with a portico in front only, *Prostyle*; with porticos at front and rear, *Amphiprostyle*; with porticos connected by open colonnades along the sides, *Peripteral*; with porticos connected only by pilasters or columns in relief, *Pseudoperipteral*; with porticos connected by double ranges of columns along the sides, *Dipteral*; with the same arrangement as regards spacing, but the inner ranges of columns omitted, *Pseudodipetral*.

TETRASTYLE See PORTCIO.

TORUS A moulding of semi-circular profile used in the bases of columns.

TRIGLYPH A feature of the frieze of the Doric order, consisting of a vertical element with two sunk vertical channels and two half-channels at the edges. The triglyph is related to the mutule above and to the guttae below. The whole system is a paraphrase in masonry of features deriving from timber construction.

TUSCAN ORDER This order derives from an ancient type of Etruscan temple and, as Vitruvius describes it, is of primitive character with wide spaces between the columns, necessarily involving timber beams. The sixteenth century theorists regarded it as proto-Doric and the crudest and most massive of the five orders.

VENETIAN WINDOW A triple opening in which the wider central opening is closed by an arch while the side openings have lintels (Fig. 2). Not characteristically Venetian but used by Bramante and Raphael, later by Scamozzi, and adopted by Inigo Jones. In English eighteenth-century practice it was common. A variant in which an outer relieving arch, concentric with the inner arch, extends over all three openings, was derived by Lord Burlington from a drawing by Palladio and used in several of his works and after him by English architects till far into the nineteenth century.

Fig. 2

VOLUTE See CAPITAL.

VOUSSOIR A block of stone, or other material, which is one of a series constituting an arch.

WATER-LEAF See ENRICHMENTS.

Notes on the Literature of Classical Architecture

Classical architecture has always, even in ancient times, depended on precedents and therefore on written treatises. Vitruvius himself declared his indebtedness to ancient authors and the classicism of the modern world has been to a great extent dependent on Vitruvius. Editions of his work therefore take precedence in any review of the literature of classical architecture. Next to Vitruvius, the treatises of sixteenth-century Italy are of the greatest consequence; they are followed by the treatises of other nations which invariably refer back both to Vitruvius and to the Italians. The following lists are highly selective and include only the best known and most representative treatises of the main European countries.

i Vitruvius

Vitruvius wrote his treatise, *de Architectura*, in the first quarter of the first century A.D. He was the only Roman writer on architecture whose work survived to be copied and re-copied through the Middle Ages. The oldest existing manuscript is in the British Museum (Harl. 2767); it belongs to the eighth century and was probably written at Jarrow. There are sixteen later medieval manuscripts in various European libraries. The first printed text appeared in Rome about 1486. The next editions were those of Fra Giocondo (Florence, 1511) and Philander (Rome, 1544). Of great importance were the illustrated translations by Cesariano (Como, 1521) and Daniele Barbaro (Venice, 1567; with illustrations by Palladio).

From the sixteenth century onwards there are translations, paraphrases and commentaries in nearly every European language, a famous if rather slight English derivative being that of Sir Henry Wotton (*Elements of Architecture*, 1624). The best modern text (with English translation) is that edited by Frank Granger for the Loeb Classical Library (Heinemann, 1931; 2nd ed. 1944–56, 2 vols.).

ii Italian Treatises

LEON BATTISTA ALBERTI (1404–1472), *De Re Aedificatoria*. Presented in MS. to Pope Nicholas V, 1452. First printed (in Latin) in Florence, 1485. The first Italian translation appeared in Venice in 1546 and the first illustrated edition in 1550. A French translation by Jean Martin followed in 1553. In England, Giacomo Leoni's translation (*Ten Books on Architecture*) appeared in 1726. A reduced facsimile of this (with introduction and notes by J. Rykwert) was published in 1955.

Alberti's treatise, although making exhaustive use of Vitruvius, is a great original work setting forth the principles of architecture in the light of the author's own philosophy and of his analysis of Roman buildings. It profoundly influenced all subsequent Italian theory.

SEBASTIANO SERLIO (1475–1552), published in his lifetime six books of architecture, all richly illustrated. In 1566, the first five were assembled as a single treatise, though not in the order they were written. The subjects of these five are (with original publication dates): 1, *Geometry* (1545); 2, *Perspective* (1545); 3, *Antiquities* (1540); 4, *The Orders* (1537); 5, *Churches* (1547). A sixth book called *Libro Estraordinario*, containing designs for arches and gateways, was published in 1551 and republished in 1566. A posthumous book made up from Serlio's drawings was published with the others at Frankfurt in 1575. The first, and only, English edition was published in 1611.

Serlio's work is both a text-book and a treasury of designs. It became the standard authority on architecture and the most popular source-book throughout Europe in the later sixteenth and seventeenth centuries, Serlio's versions of the five Orders being at the root of most expositions outside Italy, till they were superseded by Vignola and Palladio.

GIACOMO BAROZZI DA VIGNOLA (1507–1573), *Regola delli Cinque Ordini d'Architettura*, 1562. A set of fine engravings on copper of versions of the five Orders, based on Roman examples and with reference to Vitruvius. More refined and scholarly than Serlio. No text – only introduction and notes, but the book includes a number of Vignola's own designs. Many later editions, mostly Italian and French. First English edition in 1669.

ANDREA PALLADIO (1508–1580), *I Quattro Libri dell'Architettura*, Venice, 1570. The four books deal respectively with: 1, *The Orders*, 2, *Domestic Buildings* (including Palladio's own palaces and villas), 3, *Public Buildings* (mostly Roman, but including Palladio's Basilica at Vicenza) and 4, *Temples* (Roman). Palladio's orders are as refined as Vignola's. His illustrations of Roman antiquities are a great advance on Serlio's – they were, in fact, not superseded as records till Desgodetz's work of 1682. The inclusion of Palladio's own designs resulted in his recognition throughout Europe, but especially in England, as the greatest modern interpreter of classical architecture. English editions, 1663, 1715, 1736 and 1738.

VINCENZO SCAMOZZI (1552–1616), *Dell' Idea dell'Architettura Universale*, Venice, 1615. A massive work, owing much to Palladio, but designed to promote a pure, academic classicism which belongs in spirit to the eighteenth century rather than to the seventeenth.

iii *French Treatises*

PHILIBERT DE L'ORME (c. 1510–1570), *Architecture*, Paris, 1567. A work of great originality, combining thought deriving from medieval French tradition with sensitive and scholarly observation of Roman architecture.

ROLAND FRÉART (d. 1676), *Parallèle de l'Architecture Antique et de la Moderne*, Paris, 1650. A detailed critical review by a scholar, of all the established versions of the orders, ancient and modern. English edition by John Evelyn, 1664.

CLAUDE PERRAULT (1613–1688), *Ordonnances des Cinq Espèces de Colonne*, Paris, 1676. A critical dissertation on the orders with Perrault's own preferred versions (see Pl. 1). Perrault's translation of Vitruvius (Paris, 1684), with copious commentary, ranks as a treatise of major importance.

DE CORDEMOY (dates unknown), *Nouveau Traité de Toute l'Architecture*, 1706. Ostensibly concerned mostly with the orders but actually a revolutionary 'anti-Baroque' statement demanding a new purity of conception in design.

M. A. LAUGIER (1713–1769), *Essai sur l'Architecture*, Paris, 1753. Deriving mainly from Cordemoy, Laugier carries the latter's rationalism to extremes.

The above are only a few of the many French treatises. A type of great importance in the eighteenth and nineteenth centuries was that introduced by FRANÇOIS BLONDEL (1679–1719), who published his Academy lectures as *Cours d'Architecture* (Paris 1675). Other treatises based on lecture courses but encyclopaedic in character are those of A. C. D'AVILER (Paris, 1691) and JACQUES FRANÇOIS BLONDEL (Paris, 1771–1777). The *Leçons* of J. N. L. DURAND (Paris, 1801–1805 and later) reflect the severe rationalism deriving from Laugier.

iv   German and Flemish Treatises

HANS BLUM, *Quinque Columnarum exacta descriptio atque delineatio*, Zurich, 1550. An exposition of the orders based on Serlio, often republished. First English edition, 1608.

VREDEMAN DE VRIES (1527–1604), *Architectura*, Antwerp, 1577 (many later eds.). The orders, based on Serlio but elaborated and enriched (see Pl. 38).

WENDEL DIETTERLIN (*c.* 1550–1599), *Architectura*, Nuremberg, 1594–1598. Extravaganzas on the orders (see Pl. 39).

v   English Treatises

JOHN SHUTE (d. 1563), *The First and Chief Groundes of Ar-*

chitecture, London, 1563 (Facsimile, with introd. by L. Weaver, 1912). The orders, after Serlio, with variations.

JAMES GIBBS (1682–1754) *Rules for Drawing the Several Parts of Architecture*, London, 1732. An admirably clear text-book rather than a treatise.

ISAAC WARE (d. 1766), *The Complete Body of Architecture*. London, 1756. An encyclopaedic work representative of the Palladian movement.

SIR WILLIAM CHAMBERS (1723–1796), *A Treatise on Civil Architecture*, London, 1759. Republished in 1791 as *A Treatise on the Decorative Part of Civil Architecture* and again in 1825 (ed. Joseph Gwilt). A historical and critical work of great refinement.

vi   Modern Historical Works in English

For the architecture of the ancient world:

A. W. LAWRENCE, *Greek Architecture* (Pelican History of Art). Penguin Books, 1957.

D. S. ROBERTSON, *Handbook of Greek and Roman Architecture*, C.U.P., 1929. 2nd ed., 1943.

For the history of architecture since the Renaissance:

N. PEVSNER, *An Outline of European Architecture*, Penguin Books, 7th ed., 1963. The post-Renaissance chapters give an admirable general perspective, while the bibliography includes important foreign books not listed here.

R. WITTKOWER, *Architectural Principles in the Age of Humanism*, Warburg Inst., Univ. of London, 1949. Tiranti, 2nd ed., 1952.

P. MURRAY, *The Architecture of the Italian Renaissance*. Batsford, 1963.

R. WITTKOWER, *Art and Architecture in Italy 1600–1750* (Pelican History of Art). Penguin Books, 1958.

A. BLUNT, *Art and Architecture in France, 1500–1700* (Pelican History of Art). Penguin Books, 1953.

W. H. WARD, *The Architecture of the Renaissance in France,* (Vol. 1 *The Early Renaissance 1495–1640.* Vol. 2 *The Later Renaissance 1640–1830*). Batsford, 1911. 2nd ed., 1926.

J. SUMMERSON, *Architecture in Britain, 1530–1830* (Pelican History of Art). Penguin Books, 1953. 4th ed., 1963.

E. KAUFMANN, *Architecture in the Age of Reason.* Harvard U.P., 1955; O.U.P., 1955.

H. R. HITCHCOCK, *Architecture: 19th and 20th centuries* (Pelican History of Art). Penguin Books, 1958.

Monographs

J. S. ACKERMAN, *The Architecture of Michelangelo.* Zwemmer, 1961.

F. HARTT, *Giulio Romano,* 2 vols. Yale U.P., 1958; O.U.P., 1958.

W. HERRMANN, *Laugier and 18th century French Theory.* Zwemmer, 1962.

Acknowledgment is due to the following for permission to reproduce illustrations

ALBERTINA, VIENNA Plate 23; ARCHITECTURAL ASSOCIATION Plate 57; ARCHIVES PHOTOGRAPHIQUES Plate 47; B. T. BATSFORD LTD Plates 32 and 50 from *Monumental Classic Architecture* by A. E. Richardson; BILDARCHIV FOTO MARBURG Plate 30; BRITISH MUSEUM Plate 48; P. CANNON BROOKES Plate 25; CHEVOJON, PARIS Plate 63 © S.P.A.D.E.M. Paris 1963; COURTAULD INSTITUTE OF ART Plate 8; HOUSING AND ESTATES DEPT FOR YORK CITY COUNCIL Plate 20 (photo Catcheside Studio); A. F. KERSTING Plates 12, 21, 28, 46, 53 and 60; LONDON COUNTY COUNCIL Plate 51; MANSELL COLLECTION Plates 3, 9, 10, 29, 31, 41 and 45 (Anderson), 6, 7, 15, 16, 17, 27, 36, 42 and 44 (Alinari), 37 (Brogi), 43 and 54 (Giraudon); NATIONAL BUILDINGS RECORD Plates 11, 19 and 40; RADIO TIMES HULTON PICTURE LIBRARY Plate 35; ROGER SCHALL Plate 61; SIR JOHN SOANE'S MUSEUM Plate 56; THAMES AND HUDSON LTD Plate 22 from *Italian Villas and Palaces* by Georgina Masson; ULLSTEIN GMBH Plate 62; WARBURG INSTITUTE Plate 13.

We are grateful to The Royal Institute of British Architects for allowing photographs to be taken from books in their possession.

The Five orders. Pl. 1 (above): Serlio's woodcut of 1540, the
first presentation of the Orders as a complete and authoritative
series. Pl. 2 (right): Claude Perrault's version, 1676, engraved on copper, reflects the greater precision and scholarship
of its time.

2

3

4

Pl. 3 (above): the Colosseum, Rome, a major source of the 'grammar' of the Renaissance.
Pl. 4 (top right): elevation of one bay of the second (Ionic) stage of the Colosseum.
Pl. 5 (top left, opposite page): the same theme, interpreted by Vignola, 1562. In Vignola's version the interdependence of elements is such that no dimension can be changed without affecting the scale of the order and thus of the whole design.

Pl. 6 (right): the Arch of Constantine, Rome. Triumphal arches were the source of many grammatical expressions applicable to other purposes. Thus, at S. Andrea, Mantua, Pl. 7 (opposite page), Alberti, in 1472, applied the scheme of the triumphal arch to the west front of a church but replaced the attic storey by a pediment. The triumphal arch theme is again reflected in the interior, Pl. 8 (opposite page).

6

5

7

8

Pl. 8: S. Andrea, Mantua. The bay design, like the west front (Pl. 7), is based on the triumphal arch theme. Alberti here created a logical and consistent type of classical church.

The Roman circular temple and four derivatives. Pl. 9: the temple of Vesta, Rome (the entablature is missing). Pl. 10: Bramante's re-creation of the circular type at S. Pietro in Montorio, Rome, 1502. Pl. 13: dome of St Paul's (Wren, c. 1696–1708), deriving from Bramante. Pl. 11: mausoleum at Castle Howard (Hawksmoor, 1729), another derivative, with strikingly different proportions. Pl. 12: the Radcliffe Camera, Oxford (Gibbs, 1739–49), a derivative with elaborated rhythms.

9

10

11

12

Pl. 14: Bramante's House of Raphael, Rome (1512; not now existing), a High Renaissance prototype of palace façade design, consisting of a (Doric) order with coupled columns standing on an arched rusticated podium. Pl. 15: Sansovino's Palazzo Corner, Venice (1532) which repeats these elements but adds an upper storey.

16

In Palladio's buildings, antiquarian learning and artistic invention join hands. The Palazzo Chiericati, Vicenza (1551–54), Pl. 16 (left) commands a public space and the main front echoes Vitruvius's description of the galleries of a Forum while giving direct expression to the inward symmetries of a great house. Typical of Palladio is the firm articulation of the orders – Doric and Ionic. Palladio the scholar is represented again in his reconstruction of Vitruvius's 'Egyptian Hall', Pl. 18 (below), engraved in the Quattro Libri.

Pl. 17 (right): the church of Il Redentore, Venice (1576–92), by Palladio. Here the theme of Alberti's S. Andrea, Mantua (Pl. 8), is developed with a fully articulated Corinthian order. The aim of building a Christian church in Roman terms is completely fulfilled.

17

18

Palladio's authority has been accepted in many parts of the world, but especially in England. St Paul's, Covent Garden, Pl. 19 (right) is a radical study by Inigo Jones (1630) of Palladio's interpretation of the Tuscan order, with the massive eaves specified by Vitruvius but ignored by most of the theorists. In the 18th century, Palladio dominated English taste and when Lord Burlington designed the Assembly Rooms at York in 1730, he made the Ball Room, Pl. 20 (below), an exact replica of Palladio's reconstruction of the 'Egyptian Hall' (Pl. 18, opposite page). The 'Palladian' tradition in England extends as far as Sir William Chambers whose Strand front of Somerset House (1780), Pl. 21 (lower right), has the discipline and clear articulation of Palladio, though other sources are involved in its composition.

19

20

21

23

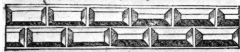

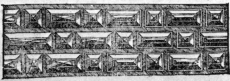

Giulio Romano and the art of Rustication. Pl. 22 (above): Cortile della Cavallerizza, Palazzo Ducale, Mantua (1538–9). Pl. 23 (top right): Giulio's drawing for the Porta Cittadella, Mantua (c. 1533). Pl. 24 (right): a page from Serlio showing various types of rusticated masonry.

24

Pl. 25: Giulio Romano's assault on the grammar of classicism. A section of the courtyard of the Palazzo del Tè, Mantua, 1526–35.

26

27

Architectural frames by Raphael and Michelangelo. Raphael's window at the Pandolfini Palace, Florence, Pl. 26, is harmonious High Renaissance prose, in which every element can be described in Vitruvian terms. The niche by Michelangelo in the Medici Chapel at S. Lorenzo, Florence, Pl. 27, is a fantasy on the same theme, manifesting an intensity of feeling which is personal. Little here can be described in Vitruvian language.

Pl. 28 (right): one of Michelangelo's twin palaces on the Capitoline Hill, Rome (1547). The giant Corinthian order embraces two storeys while an Ionic order gives expression and support to the intermediate floor. This way of combining two orders of different scales was Michelangelo's invention and a fruitful legacy to his successors. The device was used in Baroque buildings like the churches in Pls. 29 and 30 (below) and re-appears in the mid-nineteenth century Opéra in Paris (Pl. 61).

28

29

30

Two Baroque church façades which draw inspiration from the Capitoline palaces. The façade of Bernini's S. Andrea al Quirinale (1658–70), Pl. 29 (far left), is like a single bay of the Capitoline in which the Ionic order is set in motion, circuiting the oval form of the church and then swinging out through the Corinthian pilasters to make a porch. Borromini's façade of S. Carlo alle Quattro Fontane, Rome (1665–7), Pl. 30, has two orders (Ionic and Corinthian) superimposed. But in both stages a subsidiary order is related to the major order on the Capitoline principle. Bernini's fluency and Borromini's broken rhythms are well contrasted in these two treatments of the same Michelangelesque theme.

31

32

33

XXX

34

35

Pl. 34 (left): a plate from Vignola's Regola delli Cinque Ordini, showing the entablature of the Castello Farnese (Pl. 31, opposite page). This, with its vertical brackets (consoles) standing in the frieze was one of Vignola's most famous inventions, Cockerell used it, with variations, in the Sun Office (Pl. 32, opposite page) and also in the Ashmolean Museum, Oxford, Pl. 35 (above), 1841–5, a building in which Italian Mannerist artifice and Greek archeology are mixed with extraordinary subtlety.

Pl. 36 (below): the Palazzo Provinciale, Lucca by Bartolommeo Ammanati, 1577, a façade whose effect is due less to the handling of the orders than to interesting overall modelling – sunk panels, raised panels, raised panels within sunk panels and so on. In the lower storey, the purely sculptural use of the Ionic order is stressed by the two capitals 'suspended' over the haunches of the arch.

37

36

Pl. 37 (above): courtyard of the Palazzo Marino, Milan, by Galeazzo Alessi, 1558. Here, decorative carving in relief takes over almost completely from the Orders, which are manifested only in the Doric of the ground floor. In the upper storey is an 'order' of terms (pedestals with human busts) carrying an impost moulding, but it is scarcely more important than the extravagantly framed panels above or the swags and cartouches in the frieze. This conversion of architecture into decoration inspired German and Flemish designers like De Vries and Dietterlin (Pls. 38 and 39, opposite page).

Pl. 40 (right): Wollaton Hall, Nottingham, built by Robert Smythson, 1580–88. One of the most symmetrical and monumental of Elizabethan houses, it is based on a plan given by Serlio, while the ornaments derive largely from De Vries. With its great display of mullioned and transomed windows it is still very much a Tudor house, decorated rather than dominated by the display of Doric, Ionic and Corinthian pilasters.

Pls. 38 and 39 (below) are plates from two famous northern books of designs. Pl. 38 is a detail of De Vries's Corinthian Order, from his Architectura (Antwerp, 1577). Pl. 39 is a plate from the Architectura of Wendel Dietterlin (Nuremberg, 1594–8), showing terms which may be compared with those in Pl. 37 (opposite page).

38

39

40

41

43

42

Pl. 41: the Church of the Gesù, Rome, designed by Vignola in 1568 and executed by Della Porta. A façade of complex rhythms and subtle modulation, it was imitated, with every conceivable variation, throughout Europe. Two variations are illustrated here.

Pl. 42: S. Susanna, Rome, designed by Carlo Maderna in 1597. Here, the theme of the Gesù is rendered in a compact way, with decisive vertical stress, foreshadowing the Baroque.

Pl. 43 (above): the Church of the Val de Grâce, Paris, begun by François Mansart in 1645 and completed by Lemercier. Neither complex and diffuse like the Gesù, nor forceful like S. Susanna, Mansart's façade balances horizontal against vertical, projection against recession, with delicate precision.

44

45

Pl. 44 (top): St Peter's, Rome, and the Piazza.
Pl. 45 (above): Michelangelo's apse of St Peter's with
its 90 ft. high Corinthian pilasters. Pl. 46 (right):
detail of the Piazza designed by Bernini and begun in
1657.

46

Pl. 47: *east front of the Louvre, Paris, built in 1667–70 by Le Vau, Perrault and Le Brun. A complex play of influences – ancient Roman, Italian and French – here resolves itself into the greatest palace façade in Europe. The idea of coupled columns standing on a high podium goes back to Bramante (Pl. 14), but at the Louvre the Corinthian order is articulated in the spirit of a Roman temple. The division of the composition by centre and end blocks is specifically French, and so is the sculptural decoration.*

Pl. 48: Blenheim Palace, built in 1705–24 by Sir John Vanbrugh and Nicholas Hawksmoor. Compared with the solemn Louvre (opposite) Blenheim is picturesque and mobile – an affair of contrasting masses through which a major Corinthian and a subsidiary Doric order perform an elaborate counterpoint. As in the Louvre, many influences are at work. There are echoes of Palladio, Scamozzi and Bernini; but behind them all is a strong feeling for the romantic palaces of the Elizabethans.

Pl. 49 (left): A Prison Scene by Piranesi, published about 1744. This fantasy derives from the Baroque theatre but is also profoundly architectural, a romantic study in rustication. The orders are absent but the raw arches are still evocative of Rome. Piranesi made a deep impression on the imagination of the mid 18th century and prepared it for new adventures in classical design.

50

Pl. 50: old Newgate Prison, London, by George Dance, 1769 (demolished 1902). The language of rustication and the dark vision of Piranesi introduced in a building conceived as a symbol as well as a punitive stronghold.
Pl. 51: in the County Hall, London (by Ralph Knott, 1911), Piranesi is again invoked to give monumentality and prestige to the seat of an administrative body.

49

51

53

Pl. 52: the frontispiece of Laugier's Essai sur Architecture, 1753, showing the 'rustic cabin' of primitive man, 'the model upon which all the magnificences of architecture have been imagined'. The perfect building, consisting mainly of an organization of single load-bearing columns, was attempted by Soufflot in the Pantheon, Paris, Pls. 53 and 54, begun in 1756; the first great monument of Neo-classicism.

52

54

55

56

57

Pl. 55: a plate from Sir William Chambers' treatise of 1759, showing the hypothetical evolution of the Doric order from the primitive hut. A deliberate reversion to the primitive is seen in the pilaster order of Soane's Art Gallery at Dulwich (1811–14), Pl. 56.

Plain geometrical forms and archaeological purity of detail pervade the architecture of Neo-classicism. The Greek orders supersede the Roman and are reproduced undeviatingly in temple porticos and colonnades, as in Thomas Hamilton's High School at Edinburgh (1825), Pl. 57. The daring geometry of Ledoux's 'Oikema' in his ideal city (c. 1785), Pl. 58, still bows to the temple idea. Schinkel's Altes Museum in Berlin (1824–8), Pl. 59, and Smirke's British Museum (1823–47), Pl. 60, present façades which are temple peristyles unmodulated from end to end.

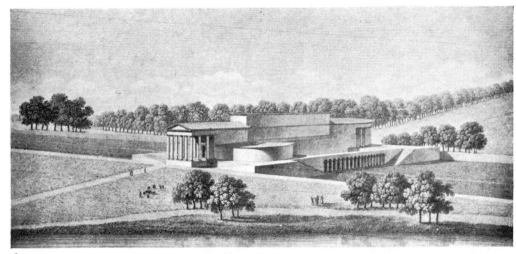

58

59

60

Pl. 61 (left): the Opéra, Paris, by Charles Garnier, 1861–75, a building in which the vocabulary of classicism is brilliantly exploited. The coupled columns on an arched podium are from Bramante, with a glance at the Louvre colonnade; the secondary order is Michelangelo's Capitoline invention; the end pavilions echo the Louvre of Lescot. The combinations are harmonious, natural to the plan and inventively enriched.

Pl. 62 (below, left): the AEG Turbine Erection Hall, Berlin, a revolutionary building by Peter Behrens, 1908, still reflects the classical temple image with pediment, colonnades and rustication in paraphrase. Pl. 63 (below, right): Auguste Perret's Naval Construction Depot, 1929, uses the device of major and subsidiary orders, though the 'orders' are never expressed, only implied in the pattern.

61

62

63